2 Corinthians

God's Sufficient Grace

*Three times I pleaded with the Lord about this, that it should leave me.
But He said to me, "My grace is sufficient for you."*

2 Corinthians 12:8–9

By Gary Dunker

CONCORDIA PUBLISHING HOUSE · SAINT LOUIS

Copyright © 2007 Concordia Publishing House

3558 S. Jefferson Ave., St. Louis, MO 63118-3968

1-800-325-3040 • www.cph.org

Written by Gary Dunker

Edited by Tim Rake

This publication may be available in braille, in large print, or on cassette tape for the visually impaired. Please allow 8 to 12 weeks for delivery. Write to Lutheran Blind Mission, 7550 Watson Rd., St. Louis, MO 63119-4409; call toll-free 1-888-215-2455; or visit the Web site: www.blindmission.org.

Manufactured in the United States of America

1 2 3 4 5 6 7 8 9 10   16 15 14 13 12 11 10 09 08 07

Contents

History	Date (AD)	2 Corinthians
Descent of the Holy Spirit in Jerusalem (Acts 2)	ca. 30	
Martyrdom of Stephen (Acts 6:8–8:1)	32	Paul's conversion and Baptism (Acts 9:1–19; 22:1–16)
Caligula Roman Emperor	37–41	
Claudius Roman Emperor	41–54	
	46–48	Paul's first missionary journey
Apostolic council in Jerusalem (Acts 15)	49–52	Paul's second missionary journey
	53–57	Paul's third missionary journey
	55–56	Paul writes 1 and 2 Corinthians
Nero Roman Emperor	54–68	
Martyrdom of James the Just	60–62	Paul under house arrest in Rome
	62–67	Paul's fourth missionary journey
Rome burns; Nero begins four-year persecution of Christians	July 9, 64	
	67	Paul imprisoned and chained in a dungeon by Nero; writes 2 Timothy (1:1–2)
Peter crucified upside down in Rome	67–68	Paul beheaded in Rome
Jerusalem captured and temple destroyed	70	
Construction begins on Roman Coliseum	71	

An Outline of 2 Corinthians

As we read through the pages of Paul's Letter, which we know today as 2 Corinthians, we are in for a special treat. Unlike any of his other Letters, in 2 Corinthians Paul personally shares with us the hardships he willingly bore as an apostle of Jesus Christ. You may recall that Christ prophetically announced that Paul "must suffer for the sake of My name" (Acts 9:16). In 2 Corinthians, we learn precisely what Christ meant by those words.

We learn of the harrowing escapes from those who sought his life, the beatings that left him perilously near death, the stoning, the sleepless nights, the hunger, and the shipwrecks. Not all of these are recorded by Luke in the Book of Acts. However, Paul endured them all so that Christ's Gospel might restore life to hearts dead in sin. Through Paul's "weakness," his Lord Jesus Christ was glorified.

We will also hear about Paul's joy in ministry and reflect on his earlier chastisements (1 Corinthians). Paul will teach us about the grace of giving. Additionally, we will marvel at Paul's humanity as he exposes his heart of love for the congregation in Corinth. We will also witness Paul's strength as he undercuts so-called "super-apostles" who would undermine his ministry during Paul's stay in Ephesus.

Following introductory material comprising 1:1–11, 2 Corinthians can be divided into three primary sections. In the first section, 1:12 through chapter 7, Paul looks back to the past. In the second, chapters 8 through 9, he looks at the present. And in the third, chapters 10 through 13, Paul looks to the future. Paul will close his Letter with a trinitarian benediction of Jesus' grace, God's love, and the Spirit's fellowship.

I. The God of All Comfort (1:1–11)
    A. Greetings from Paul and Timothy (1:1, 2)
    B. Comforted by God to Comfort Others (1:3–7)
    C. Paul's Hardships (1:8–11)
II. Paul Looks Back—Why Paul Changed His Plans and the Glory of His Ministry (1:12–7:16)
    A. Paul's Dealings with the Corinthians (1:12–2:13)

Introduction

By our standards, Paul's mission was impossible: convert the Corinthians to faith in Jesus Christ. We can only imagine how difficult this was for Paul in a city whose name symbolized drunkenness and debauchery—even among their fellow Greeks.

Located on the isthmus connecting Peloponese with Greece, Corinth thrived on its reputation as a major trade center of the Roman Empire. Ships docked at three Corinthian harbors and citizens flocked in from throughout the ancient world. Cargo-laden ships were unloaded on one side of the isthmus and the cargo was carried by hand to the other side, where it was loaded on a second vessel. Approximately five hundred thousand people made Corinth their home in the first century AD, a far cry from its humble reestablishment under Julius Caesar only a century before.

Among Corinth's citizenry were dockworkers, merchants, sailors, gamblers, athletes, and slaves. Prostitution, both male and female, was rampant. Overlooking the Corinthian landscape stood the Acro-corinthus. This natural landmark rose some two thousand feet above the southwest part of the city. On its apex stood the infamous Temple of Aphrodite, with its thousand prostitutes pouring "religious" pestilence into a notoriously heathen city. Nearly five hundred meters north of Corinth, archeologists discovered a second sanctuary, dedicated to Asklepios. Here, evidence dating back to the time of Paul (circa AD 50) was uncovered. Sin abounded while morality seemed nonexistent.

Into this hostile environment, God sent the apostle Paul (Acts 18:9–10). Finding little support for his ministry among the Jews, Paul turned his attention to the Gentiles (Acts 18:6) and devoted nearly a year and a half to God's work there. During that time, Paul gathered a congregation of both Jews and Gentiles. The Lord worked wonders through Paul as he modeled Christ for them. More importantly, the Corinthians could see Christ in the cross-shaped form of Paul's life and ministry. Now, in Paul's absence, this first-century congregation—and Paul himself—came under attack from within, with their enemies threatening to sever the very cords that bound them together. An earlier letter of chastisement, the Letter we know as 1 Corinthians, was sent with Titus and others. As Christ brought reconciliation between God and man, Paul sought to apply that same reconciliation to the lives of the Corinthians. Now, a second letter was needed. How would the Holy Spirit respond through Paul? Let's begin our journey through 2 Corinthians.

Lesson 1

The God of All Comfort

2 Corinthians belongs to an ancient collection of thirteen New Testament Letters written by the apostle Paul. These Letters are known as the "Pauline Epistles." Besides 2 Corinthians, the other Letters from Paul are Romans, 1 Corinthians, Galatians, Ephesians, Philippians, Colossians, 1 and 2 Thessalonians, 1 and 2 Timothy, Titus, and Philemon. Paul wrote 2 Corinthians while in Macedonia (2:13; 7:5). According to many historians, the year was about AD 56.

Of Paul's Letters, 2 Corinthians is the most autobiographical, providing personal information not found in any other Letter or even in the Book of Acts, which highlights Paul's missionary work. In 2 Corinthians, we learn that Paul was a Hebrew (2 Corinthians 11:22); that he was imprisoned and severely flogged (v. 23); that he received forty lashes minus one five times at the hands of the Jews (v. 24); and that was beaten by rods, stoned, and shipwrecked three times (v. 25). We also learn of Paul's infirmity, a "thorn in the flesh," that was so painful that three times Paul asked God to remove it (12:8). Paul does not provide these details lightly. He is not trying to elicit sympathy from his Corinthian readers or any other congregation in Greece where this Letter might have circulated. Rather, Paul is simply chronicling events in his life to show how God triumphed through his weaknesses (11:30). Paul knows firsthand of God's comfort for those He loves in Christ, and he recalls that comfort as he dictates this Letter to a congregation that he dearly loves.

Setting the Stage

Paul established a Christian congregation in Corinth about AD 51, during his second missionary journey (Acts 18:1–18). We know that, while ministering in Ephesus during his third missionary journey (ca. AD 53–57), Paul traveled across the Aegean Sea to visit Corinth a second time. (Paul mentions an impending third visit in 2 Corinthians 12:14 and 13:1–2.) This second visit was the "painful visit" Paul addresses in 2 Corinthians 2:1. After his second visit, Paul wrote a second Letter to the Corinthians, stating, "I wrote to you in my letter not to associate with sexually immoral people" (1 Corinthians 5:9).

1. Read 1 Corinthians 1:11–12. What were the ongoing problems in Corinth that came to Paul's attention after his second visit and his first Letter?

2. Read 1 Corinthians 5:9–11; 6:1; and 8:4. What additional problems in Corinth do these passages bring to light?

Paul's Third Letter

Paul originally planned to travel across the Aegean Sea to visit the Corinthians. Instead, he took the overland route, passing through Troas and on into Macedonia. While in Macedonia, Titus brought news of his visit to Corinth (2 Corinthians 7:5–7). Although this is Paul's third Letter to the Corinthians, only his second and third Letters survive, which are 1 and 2 Corinthians respectively.

3. Read 2 Corinthians 1:1. In Paul's day, letters began with an introduction of the writer, a listing of persons on hand at the time of the writing, and a notice of the intended recipient(s). From this passage, locate each of these three common components of a first century AD letter.

4. Read Acts 19:15–16. By whose authority can Paul consider himself an apostle? How does Paul attest this authority in 2 Corinthians 1:1?

5. In 2 Corinthians 1:2, Paul continues his introduction with an apostolic blessing. Are these words merely Paul's pious sentiment, or do they convey something more?

God's Comfort

Read 2 Corinthians 1:3 and then compare the passage to Romans 1:8; 1 Corinthians 1:4; Ephesians 1:15–16; and Colossians 1:3. These five verses include the introductory material found in most Pauline Letters.

6. How did Paul typically begin his Letters? How might the absence of this introductory material in 2 Corinthians be related to the specific problems encountered by the congregation in Corinth?

7. Read 2 Corinthians 1:4–11. As you do, count the number of times Paul uses the word *comfort*. Why do you think Paul's frequent use of this word is important?

8. How does Paul point to his own life as an example of God's grace and comfort? What is the gist of Paul's statement about God raising the dead? What does that mean for you and me?

9. Why do you believe Paul put such an emphasis on the prayers others were making for him? Do we likewise need others to pray for us?

God's Word for Today

All Christians experience disappointments, trials, tragedies, and other forms of suffering. Most of us, however, will never experience the sufferings Paul experienced for the sake of the Gospel of Jesus Christ.

10. Paul was able to comfort others, because he received comfort from God. Think about those who comforted you in your time of trial. How might God use you to comfort others?

11. What are some ways that God provides us a "way of escape" (1 Corinthians 10:13)?

12. Elsewhere, Paul noted that "through many tribulations we must enter the kingdom of God" (Acts 14:22) and that "all things work together for good, for those who are called according to His purpose"

(Romans 8:28). If you feel comfortable, share a time when God worked together for His good purpose during a troubling time in your life.

In Closing

Encourage participants to begin the following activities:
* Consult a Bible concordance for additional Bible verses referencing God's comfort for us in Christ. Make a list of these passages, and affix them on an object you see every day, such as your refrigerator or computer monitor.
* Consider how Christ is the Yes! to all of God's promises.
* Read 2 Corinthians 1:12–2:13 to prepare for the next lesson.

Speak or sing together the following stanzas of "Abide with Me" (*LSB* 878; *LW* 490).

Abide with me, fast falls the eventide.
The darkness deepens; Lord, with me abide.
When other helpers fail and comforts flee,
Help of the helpless, O abide with me.

I need Thy presence ev'ry passing hour;
What but Thy grace can foil the tempter's pow'r?
Who like Thyself my guide and stay can be?
Through cloud and sunshine, O abide with me.

Come not in terrors, as the King of kings,
But kind and good, with healing in Thy wings;
Tears for all woes, a heart for ev'ry plea.
Come, Friend of sinners, thus abide with me.

Swift to its close ebbs out life's little day;
Earth's joys grow dim, its glories pass away;
Change and decay in all around I see;
O Thou who changest not, abide with me.

I fear no foe with Thee at hand to bless;
Ills have no weight and tears no bitterness.
Where is death's sting? Where, grave, thy victory?
I triumph still if Thou abide with me!

Hold Thou Thy cross before my closing eyes;
Shine through the gloom, and point me to the skies.
Heav'n's morning breaks, and earth's vain shadows flee;
In life, in death, O Lord, abide with me.

Lesson 2

God's Answer Is Yes!

Paul faced opposition among Jewish religious leaders in Corinth. This opposition became so fierce that Paul "left the synagogue" to establish a church next door in the home of Titius Justus (Acts 18:6–7). At this point, we surmise that the relationship between Paul and the Corinthians was untroubled. Paul "stayed a year and six months, teaching the word of God among them" (Acts 18:11). Later, "Paul stayed many days longer and then took leave of the brothers" in order to sail to Ephesus (Acts 18:18–19). Sadly, in Paul's absence, the little Corinthian congregation began to eat itself from within.

With Paul away, Satan incited conflicts the young congregation was ill prepared to handle: a parishioner in an incestuous relationship (1 Corinthians 5:1); frivolous lawsuits (6:1–2); a cavalier attitude toward sexual immorality (vv. 16–17); and church members who taught that remaining unmarried made them better equipped to serve the Church (7:1). There were also fights concerning the eating of food sacrificed to pagan idols (8:1) and questions over Paul's authority to call himself an apostle (9:1–2). Individuals within the Corinthian congregation begin to criticize Paul for being hard to understand, untrustworthy, and too harsh.

First Charge: Paul Is Hard to Understand

If Paul were discredited, the Gospel message would have been obscured. Results might have been that the Corinthians lost their faith and that the church in Corinth, in a city known for vice and division, was scandalized.

Read 2 Corinthians 1:12–14.

13. What charge did some of the Corinthians make against Paul (v. 13)? At times, Paul's words may appear difficult to understand (even Peter recognized this; see 2 Peter 3:16–17). However, they

16

always revolve around one simple truth. What is it (see Ephesians 1:7–8)?

14. In spite of their charges, what does Paul desire for the congregation's members (2 Corinthians 1:14)? How is it possible to acknowledge Paul in part, and then later to acknowledge him fully? Why would Paul desire that the Corinthians "boast" in him as he "boasts" in them?

Second Charge: Paul Is Untrustworthy

Paul's Letter also shows that he is countering a charge of untrustworthiness. Most likely, this accusation arose because Paul had changed his travel plans, which his adversaries had twisted to imply that Paul's message could no longer be trusted.

Read 2 Corinthians 1:15–24.

15. Describe a time when someone accused you of being untrustworthy. How did these attacks make you feel? Angry? Hurt? Did you want to lash back at your accusers? Explain.

16. What was Paul's original plan for his third visit to Corinth? Why did Paul change his mind?

17. Which concerned Paul more: that the Corinthians believe the Gospel message or that they believe his explanation of the changes to his itinerary? What leads you to your conclusion?

18. How are God's promises to us always Yes in Christ? What allowed the Corinthians to remain firm in the faith that Paul and others had proclaimed to them?

Third Charge: Paul Is Too Harsh

In spite of the false accusations of some of the Corinthians, Paul exposed his heart to them. He wrote candidly and lovingly to these his spiritual children, much like a father would write to a beloved son or daughter.

Read 2 Corinthians 2:1–11.

19. Why did Paul travel indirectly to Corinth?

20. Read 1 Corinthians 5:1–5; 6:5. Paul made his second missionary visit to Corinth prior to writing 1 Corinthians. Does Paul sound harsh in these passages? Why or why not?

21. What does Paul teach the Corinthians about Satan (2 Corinthians 2:11)? Two of Satan's temptations are to encourage us (a) to ignore sin (or to approve it!) or (b) to withhold forgiveness from

18

someone who is repentant. Why should we be careful to apply both Law and Gospel when dealing with sin?

God's Word for Today

In dealing with sin in their midst, congregations and pastors apply both Law and Gospel: Law for the unrepentant sinner and Gospel for the repentant sinner. The goal of this application is always restoration and forgiveness.

22. How does Paul apply Law and Gospel in the case of the incestuous relationship brought to light in 1 Corinthians? What verses in 2 Corinthians support your answer?

23. In his earlier Letter, Paul demanded that the incestuous member be excommunicated (1 Corinthians 5:1–2, 4–5, 13). Ultimately, however, what is the purpose of such excommunication (2 Corinthians 2:5–11)?

24. How are Paul's actions a modeling of Christ's words found in Luke 17:3–4?

In Closing

Encourage participants to begin the following activities:

- Examine how on the cross Christ offered forgiveness to the two thieves and how the Law and the Gospel are both presented (Luke 23:38–43).
- Discuss Paul's conviction that it is more important to believe God than man.
- Read 2 Corinthians 2:12–4:6 to prepare for the next session.

Speak or sing together the following stanzas of "Chief of Sinners Though I Be" (*LSB* 611; *LW* 285).

Chief of sinners though I be,
Jesus shed His blood for me,
Died that I might live on high,
Lives that I might never die.
As the branch is to the vine,
I am His, and He is mine.

Oh, the height of Jesus' love,
Higher than the heav'ns above,
Deeper than the depths of sea,
Lasting as eternity!
Love that found me—wondrous thought!
Found me when I sought Him not.

Only Jesus can impart
Balm to heal the wounded heart,
Peace that flows from sin forgiv'n,
Joy that lifts the soul to heav'n,
Faith and hope to walk with God
In the way that Enoch trod.

Chief of sinners though I be,
Christ is all in all to me;
All my wants to Him are known,
All my sorrows are His own.
He sustains the hidden life
Safe with Him from earthly strife.

O my Savior, help afford
By Your Spirit and Your Word!
When my wayward heart would stray,
Keep me in the narrow way;
Grace in time of need supply
While I live and when I die.

Lesson 3

Superiority of the New Covenant

What was so special about the Gospel that Paul presented? What was it that allowed him to willingly face beatings, shipwrecks, and stoning with unwavering faith? How could men such as Paul and Timothy offer the Gospel, or Good News, without hesitation to Jew and Gentile alike?

Long before Christ lived out His earthly mission, God promised Adam and Eve that He would provide a Savior from sin (Genesis 3:15). Later, God made a covenant with Abraham and promised him that he would be the father of many nations through his Seed (Genesis 12:1–7; 13:14–17; 15:1–6; see also Galatians 3:15–29). Four hundred and thirty years later, in order to make His people aware of their discordant and disobedient lives, God provided His Law on stone tablets, which stipulated how His people were to live in harmony with Him and with each other (Exodus 20:1–17).

In his Letter to the Romans, Paul explained the primary purpose of God's Law: "Through the law comes knowledge of sin" (Romans 3:20) and awareness that "the wages of sin is death" (Romans 6:23). The Old Testament rites and ceremonies that God instituted foreshadowed the ultimate sacrifice Jesus would make for the sins of the world (see Hebrews 10:1–18). It is Jesus' new covenant (see Hebrews 9:15–28) that Jesus announces to His disciples when they are gathered for the Last Supper (Matthew 26:26–28). In Christ and through the shedding of His holy blood, humankind has been reconciled to God. To Paul, that's worth dying for.

Paul in Macedonia

Traveling overland to Corinth allowed Paul a short return visit to Troas. Five or six years earlier, Paul had received a vision there of a man begging him to come to Macedonia (Acts 16:8–10). Paul waited at Troas for Titus to bring word of the Corinthians' response to Paul's Letter (1 Corinthians) and Titus's subsequent visit. When Titus did not arrive at the agreed-upon time, Paul pressed on to Macedonia.

Read 2 Corinthians 2:12–13.

25. Paul expressed his deep concern for the Corinthian congregation and how they might react to his "painful visit" and follow-up Letter (2 Corinthians 2:1–2, 9). What was he hoping Titus's presence would bring him?

26. Sharing optional. Discuss a time when you made a "painful" but necessary remark and spent a sleepless night wondering about its repercussions. How did God comfort you while you awaited the outcome?

The New Covenant's Superiority

Read 2 Corinthians 2:14–17. In the first century AD, Roman generals were sometimes given a *triumph*, a victorious parade through Rome to honor their conquest. Behind the general riding in his chariot were the vanquished, led in chains. In this portion of 2 Corinthians, Paul draws upon Corinthians' knowledge of this spectacle and uses it as an "object lesson" of Christ's victory.

27. If Paul writes that God "leads us in triumphal procession" in Christ, who are the vanquished?

28. Read Psalm 46:6. In Luther's "A Mighty Fortress Is Our God," we sing, "One little word subdues him [Satan]." Although many have speculated about what Luther's "one little word" might be, how might *tetelestai,* the final word Jesus spoke from the cross ("It is finished" [John 19:30]), serve as the "voice" that melts the earth, the "word" that subdues the devil?

29. How does Paul contrast his work among the Corinthians with that of the false apostles who had sought to influence them (2 Corinthians 2:17)?

Read 2 Corinthians 3:1–18.
30. How were the Corinthians like Paul's letter of recommendation or "a letter from Christ"?

31. In his sacristy prayer, Martin Luther confessed, "If I am left to myself, I will certainly bring it all to destruction." How did Paul and Luther recognize their own weaknesses? How do we?

32. In 2 Corinthians 3:1–11, Paul draws a sharp contrast between the ministry of Moses (the Law) and the ministry of Christ (the Gospel). From the verses in this chapter, determine if the following refer to either Law or Gospel:
    a.   a letter written . . . on tablets of stone (v. 3);

b. a letter written on human hearts (v. 3);

c. ministry "of the letter" (v. 6);

d. ministry "of a new covenant" (v. 6);

e. the letter that "kills" (v. 6);

f. the Spirit that "gives life" (v. 6);

g. the "ministry of death" (v. 7);

h. the "ministry of the Spirit" (v. 8);

i. the "ministry of condemnation" (v. 9);

j. the "ministry of righteousness" (v. 9);

k. the glory that is no longer (v. 10);

l. the glory that is permanent (v. 11).

Read 2 Corinthians 4:1–6.

33. Paul set forth the Gospel plainly in his teaching and preaching. However, to some the Gospel remained "veiled." List some of the many ways that the Gospel is "veiled" by "the god of this world" (Satan [v. 4]).

God's Word for Today

Jesus is "the image of God" (2 Corinthians 4:4) in human flesh, because He is the Word made flesh (John 1:1–2, 14; Colossians 1:15–20). Through Baptism, God began restoring His image in us (Colossians 2:9–15; 3:1–10), the image that we lost in the fall.

34. Christ's servants like Paul preach "Jesus Christ as Lord, with [themselves] as . . . servants for Jesus' sake" (2 Corinthians 4:5). Through the preaching of the Gospel of Christ, God restores His image in us. What obligation do Gospel hearers have toward Gospel preachers (see 1 Thessalonians 5:12–13; Hebrews 13:17)?

35. At creation, God created light out of darkness (Genesis 1:2–4). When He recreates us, He shines His light into our hearts through the Gospel (2 Corinthians 4:6). What are some ways that we, as individuals and congregations, can let our "light shine before others" (see Matthew 5:14–16)?

36. The glory of the new covenant is the "glory of God in the face of Jesus Christ" (2 Corinthians 4:6). How does everything else—the world and all its allures—pale by comparison?

In Closing

Encourage participants to begin the following activities:
• Reread God's seven-fold promise to Abraham found in

Genesis 12:2–3, and rejoice that we are Abraham's spiritual children through faith in his Seed, our Savior, Jesus Christ.

- Give thanks to God for shining the light of Christ into your heart through the Gospel.
- Read 2 Corinthians 4:7–5:10 to prepare for the next session.

Speak or sing together the following stanzas of "Jesus Lives! The Victory's Won" (*LSB* 490; *LW* 139).

Jesus lives! The vict'ry's won!
    Death no longer can appall me;
Jesus lives! Death's reign is done!
    From the grave will Christ recall me.
Brighter scenes will then commence;
This shall be my confidence.

Jesus lives! To Him the throne
    High above all things is given.
I shall go where He is gone,
    Live and reign with Him in heaven.
God is faithful; doubtings, hence!
This shall be my confidence.

Jesus lives! For me He died,
    Hence will I, to Jesus living,
Pure in heart and act abide,
    Praise to Him and glory giving.
All I need God will dispense;
This shall be my confidence.

Jesus lives! I know full well
    Nothing me from Him shall sever.
Neither death nor pow'rs of hell
    Part me now from Christ forever.
God will be my sure defense;
This shall be my confidence.

Jesus lives! And now is death
    But the gate of life immortal;
This shall calm my trembling breath
    When I pass its gloomy portal.
Faith shall cry, as fails each sense:
Jesus is my confidence!

Lesson 4

Treasure in Clay Jars

Archeologists have traced the beginnings of pottery making to an area between the Tigris and Euphrates Rivers some eight thousand years ago. Solid clay containers, many made without the use of a potter's wheel, were created in order to store grain. Later, about 2500 BC, the eastern coast of the Mediterranean saw the advent of a *slow-turning* potter's wheel. However, it was the Greeks who revolutionized pottery when they invented the *fast-turning* potter's wheel. This invention revolutionized the art of sophisticated pottery making, nearly a millennium before Paul carried the Gospel to Corinth.

For a period of about two hundred years (750–550 BC), Corinth was a primary producer of the fine pottery used throughout the Mediterranean and Black Sea areas. Some Corinthian pottery even made its way into France, Germany, and Hungary. However, beginning about 570 BC, Athens supplanted Corinth as the leading manufacturer of exquisite pottery. As we will see, Paul was obviously familiar with Grecian pottery, for he makes use of it as a figure of the Christian life.

The Potter and the Clay

In a master potter's practiced hands, a shapeless lump of clay is turned into a practical and beautiful vessel. The lump is smoothed and centered atop the wheel head. Seasoned thumbs skillfully apply exacting pressure to open up the clay to the master's desired shape. The potter applies his skill and attention to the piece, and in response the lump yields itself and becomes a serviceable and lovely product.

37. Describe some of the difficulties and satisfactions gained by

an artistic endeavor such as "throwing" clay, woodworking, quilting, or painting.

38. After firing, glazing, and firing a second time, a clay vessel becomes functional. However, is it unbreakable?

Paul's *Jars of Clay* Metaphor

Read 2 Corinthians 4:7–18. Paul has just concluded a section of his Letter glorifying the superiority of the new covenant over the old.

39. To what does Paul contrast the glory of the new covenant message?

40. As the potter shapes the clay, who shapes the messenger for useful service?

41. How has God formed and shaped Paul as a messenger of the Gospel?

42. John the Baptist said of Christ, "He must increase, but I must decrease" (John 3:30). How did Paul also "decrease" for the sake of Christ and His Gospel (2 Corinthians 4:11)?

43. The Holy Spirit used Paul, a fragile jar of clay, for a noble purpose, that is, to share the Gospel (v. 15). How is this restated in Paul's Letter to Timothy (1 Timothy 2:3–4)?

Paul's Heavenly Dwelling

In addition to *jars of clay*, Paul uses another metaphor to contrast earthly existence with heavenly existence.

Read 2 Corinthians 5:1–10.

44. Why might Paul's tent metaphor have personal significance for him (see Acts 18:3)?

45. What is the similarity between clay jars and earthly tents?

46. For what does Paul long (2 Corinthians 5:4–5)? In spite of human frailties, what is Paul's attitude on life (v. 6)?

God's Word for Today

Paul writes that he "walk[s] by faith, not by sight" (2 Corinthians 5:7). His life served as a witness to faith that trusts in Christ's merits and not his own.

47. In spite of many hardships, Paul's life was filled with constant hope. How does a living faith, produced by the Holy Spirit through the Gospel, preserve us from a Christian life that is overtaken by doubt or that is morose or sorrowful?

48. In 2 Corinthians 5:10, Paul returns to a theme found in 1 Corinthians 3:11–15. For what will all people, believers and unbelievers alike, have to give an account on the Last Day?

In Closing

Encourage participants to begin the following activities:
- Think about ways you might put Paul's message of 2 Corinthians 5:6–7 into practice.
- Personally reflect on ways God might use you, a fragile jar of clay, in furthering His kingdom.
- Read 2 Corinthians 6:11–7:4 to prepare for the next session.

Speak or sing together the following stanzas of "I Walk in Danger All the Way" (*LSB* 716:1, 2, 5, 6; *LW* 391:1, 2, 5, 6).

I walk in danger all the way.
    The thought shall never leave me
That Satan, who has marked his prey,
    Is plotting to deceive me.
        This foe with hidden snares
        May seize me unawares
If I should fail to watch and pray.
I walk in danger all the way.

I pass through trials all the way,
    With sin and ills contending;
In patience I must bear each day
    The cross of God's own sending.
        When in adversity
        I know not where to flee,
When storms of woe my soul dismay,
I pass through trials all the way.

I walk with Jesus all the way,
　His guidance never fails me;
Within His wounds I find a stay
　When Satan's pow'r assails me;
　　　And by His footsteps led,
　　　My path I safely tread.
　No evil leads my soul astray;
　I walk with Jesus all the way.

My walk is heav'nward all the way;
　Await, my soul, the morrow,
When God's good healing shall allay
　All suff'ring, sin, and sorrow.
　　　Then, worldly pomp, begone!
　　　To heav'n I now press on.
　For all the world I would not stay;
　My walk is heav'nward all the way.

Lesson 5

Ministry of Reconciliation

It has been said, "God doesn't call the equipped; He equips the called." These words fit Saul of Tarsus, whom we know by his Roman name, *Paul*. If ever God turned a life in an opposite direction, it was Saul's.

Reared as a devout Jew and trained under the noted Rabbi Gamaliel, Saul defended the Jewish faith against all challengers. He had heard Stephen call to Christ for mercy on behalf of those who stoned him (Acts 7:59–60). But he wasn't prepared to meet Jesus face-to-face. The road to Damascus changed everything.

After encountering the risen Lord, Paul's assignment became that of carrying the name of Jesus Christ to the Gentiles and their kings, in addition to the Jews (Acts 9:15). Instead of carrying credentials given by the Sanhedrin, Saul now carried the oral proclamation of Christ: that God was reconciling sinful humanity to Himself in Christ, "not counting [men's] trespasses against them" (2 Corinthians 5:19).

Another Charge against Paul

In our second lesson, we discussed three charges that certain individuals leveled against Paul: (1) he was hard to understand, (2) he was untrustworthy, and (3) he was too harsh. In the opening verse of today's lesson (2 Corinthians 5:11), we encounter a fourth charge. Some Corinthians argued that, since Paul was not among those who walked with Christ, he was not a true apostle, but a pretender. For the sake of the Gospel, Paul felt compelled to defend his calling.

49. Review 2 Corinthians 5:10. That all people will give an account to God on the Last Day reassures Paul. Why?

50. Paul appeals to his actions while living among the Corinthians as proof of his ministry. What was Paul trying to do while living there?

Paul's Defense

Read 2 Corinthians 5:11–19. While Paul tries to persuade others (v. 11), Christ Himself knows that Paul is His chosen apostle. For Paul, human opinion is irrelevant; all is Christ (vv. 13–15).

51. From these verses, discuss why Paul would be willing to suffer ridicule, mockery, beatings, stonings, and imprisonment (see also 2 Corinthians 11:23–29).

52. Does Paul seem concerned about how the Corinthians perceive him? What is Paul's chief concern and what compels him to view life this way?

53. What does Paul mean when he writes, "we regard no one according to the flesh" (2 Corinthians 5:16)? What brings forth the "new creation" that Paul writes about (v. 17; see also Titus 3:5–8)?

54. What is Paul's overriding defense, and what is the ministry Paul brings to the Corinthians (see also Romans 5:10; Ephesians 2:16; Colossians 1:20–22)?

Paul's Ministry of Reconciliation

Paul has described himself as "an apostle of Christ Jesus by the will of God" (2 Corinthians 1:1) and a minister "of a new covenant" (3:6). Now, as God's chosen representative, Paul notes that he is Christ's "ambassador" (5:20). "In the stead and by the command of [his] Lord Jesus Christ" (*Lutheran Service Book*, p. 185), Paul implores the Corinthians for Christ's sake.

Read 2 Corinthians 5:20–6:13.

55. What word does Paul use to describe the task Christ has given him (v. 20)? What does that word mean? Explain how the Corinthians might receive God's grace in vain (6:1)?

56. How was Paul known among the Corinthians (6:3–10)?

57. How does Paul express his deepest emotions for the Corinthians (vv. 11–12)? How does he feel toward them (v. 13)?

Unequal Yoking

By separating themselves from their spiritual father and his teachings, the Corinthians were also joining in the fellowship of unbelief. According to Old Testament ceremonial law, a "clean" ox could not be yoked together with an "unclean" donkey (Deuteronomy 22:10). Paul draws upon this analogy to warn his children in the faith not to join in the worship of unbelievers.

Read 2 Corinthians 6:14–7:1.

58. While Christians will have contact with unbelievers in this world (see 1 Corinthians 5:10), why should believers avoid coming under the influence of false teachings or false teachers?

59. Some Christian scholars have applied Paul's words about not being "yoked with unbelievers" to marriage, teaching that believers should not marry unbelievers. However, what did Paul recommend to Christian spouses who were already married to unbelievers (1 Corinthians 7:12–16)?

God's Word for Today

Many world religions promise a moral guide to living, a better existence here or in the hereafter, or just a worldview to help their adherents "get by." However, the message of the Christian faith and the ministry of Paul and all pastors in Christ is that God has reconciled the world to Himself in Christ.

60. Using a dictionary or a Bible dictionary (if available), define the word *reconcile*. What does *reconciliation* mean in terms of a believer's relationship to God? What practical steps can you take to encourage reconciliation within your family? your congregation?

61. In his earlier Letter (1 Corinthians 6:19), Paul noted that each individual Christian is a "temple" of the Holy Spirit. In 2 Corinthians 6:16, Paul calls the congregation "the temple of the living God." How do congregations give expression to this unseen unity?

In Closing

Encourage participants to begin the following activities:

- In 2 Corinthians 6:16–18, Paul quotes Isaiah 52:11; Ezekiel 20:34, 41; and 2 Samuel 7:8, 14). Review the context of these passages to gain insight into Paul's words to the Corinthians.
- Discuss how you might have felt had you been among the parishioners receiving Paul's Letter and hearing the words of 2 Corinthians 6:3–10 read aloud.
- Read 2 Corinthians 7:2–7:16 to prepare for the next session.

Speak or sing together the words of "Through Jesus' Blood and Merit" (*LSB* 746; *LW* 369). Notice how the opening words speak of God's reconciling the world to Himself.

Through Jesus' blood and merit
  I am at peace with God.
What, then, can daunt my spirit,
  However dark my road?
My courage shall not fail me,
  For God is on my side;
Though hell itself assail me,
  Its rage I may deride.

There's nothing that can sever
  From this great love of God;
No want, no pain whatever,
  No famine, peril, flood.
Though thousand foes surround me,
  For slaughter mark His sheep,
They never shall confound me,
  The vict'ry I shall reap.

For neither life's temptation
  Nor death's most trying hour
Nor angels of high station
  Nor any other pow'r
Nor things that now are present
  Nor things that are to come
Nor height, however pleasant,
  Nor darkest depths of gloom

Nor any creature ever
    Shall from the love of God
This ransomed sinner sever;
    For in my Savior's blood
This love has its foundation;
    God hears my faithful prayer
And long before creation
    Named me His child and heir.

Lesson 6

Paul and Titus

Titus was more than Paul's traveling companion; he was a devout follower of Christ. Titus traveled with Paul and Barnabas to Antioch and accompanied them to the Council in Jerusalem (see Galatians 2:1–5). Titus was a Greek Gentile whom Paul refused to circumcise, even though the Judaizers (those who insisted that Christians strictly follow the Jewish ceremonial law) insisted Paul do so (Galatians 2:3). Titus was with Paul and Timothy at Ephesus (see 2 Corinthians 2:13).

As we will learn in this session, Paul enjoyed and drew much strength from working with his colleague Titus. Later, we will learn that Titus was sent to Corinth to collect contributions for the poor Christians in Jerusalem (2 Corinthians 8:6; 12:18). We will also learn that Titus carried the Letter we now know as 2 Corinthians to the congregation there (8:16–17). Little mention is made of Titus following his reunion with Paul in Macedonia until Paul writes the Epistle to Titus. Tradition holds that Titus died on Crete about AD 107, at about the age of 95.

62. It has been said that "there is strength in numbers." How might fellow co-workers in the Gospel be a source of strength?

63. When Jesus sent out the seventy-two (Luke 10:1–3; see also 9:1–6; Mark 6:7), He sent them out in pairs. The Early Church continued this practice (see Acts 13:2; 15:27, 39–40; 17:14; 19:22). When it comes to ministry, what are some benefits of not "going it alone"?

Paul Rejoices over the Corinthians

Read 2 Corinthians 7:2–4. Although Paul may sometimes sound harsh when he writes, he is not without true compassion for the congregation in Corinth.

64. In this passage, how does Paul express his love for the Corinthians? In what ways does Paul reflect Christ's compassion for all sinners (John 15:13; Romans 5:6–8)?

65. In spite of harsh circumstances in his life as an apostle, how is Paul able to be "bold," to take godly "pride" in the Corinthians, and to be "filled with comfort" and "overflowing with joy" (2 Corinthians 7:4)? If you feel comfortable, share how God has helped you in the midst of troubling conflict.

Paul and Titus Reunite

Read 2 Corinthians 7:5–16. In this passage, we learn why Paul was able to rejoice (7:4) and we hear more about his travels (he stopped writing about them in 2:13). The reaction of the Corinthian congregation to his first Letter and his subsequent "painful visit" (2:1) was now relayed to him by Titus, whom Paul already had sent ahead of him to Corinth.

66. What word does Titus bring that stirs rejoicing in Paul's heart (7:7)? Whom does Paul credit for these comforting words?

67. How do verses 8–10 show that, while Paul was a devout man of God and Christ's chosen apostle, Paul was also human, just like you and me?

68. How does Paul differentiate godly grief, which results in repentance and faith, from worldly grief, which results only in bitter regret and death?

End of Class

69. In verse 11, Paul commends the Corinthians for their "godly grief." List what this God-inspired sorrow has produced in the Corinthians.

70. In verse 11, "fear" may be interpreted as "reverence," and "punishment" may be understood as "eagerness to see justice carried out." In what ways does genuine repentance also inspire and enable a change in thoughts and feelings?

71. How was Titus himself refreshed by the godly spirit of the Corinthians (vv. 13, 15)?

72. As you think about the attitude of the Corinthians toward God's message of love delivered by Paul, what word or words come to mind? How do we experience this in our lives as well?

God's Word for Today

It is easy to receive a positive, uplifting message from God's chosen servants. It may even be easy to receive correction and rebuke from them. However, it is often very difficult to correct or rebuke

42

someone ourselves. Nevertheless, when it comes to church discipline, however, God means it for our good.

73. In your opinion, were the Corinthians in need of Paul's chastisement and church discipline?

74. How do Paul's words, found in today's lesson, remind us that if we as a congregation really love someone we should offer him or her loving discipline so that he or she might be restored to Christ and His Church?

In Closing

Encourage participants to begin the following activities:
- Review the steps for the administration of church discipline as Christ details them in Matthew 18:15–17.
- Discuss how God comforted (1) the Corinthian church, (2) the man in an incestuous relationship, and (3) Paul and Titus through the process of church discipline.
- Read 2 Corinthians 8:1–9:15 to prepare for the next session.

Say or sing together the words of "Lord, to You I Make Confession" (*LSB* 608; *LW* 233).

Lord, to You I make confession:
    I have sinned and gone astray,
I have multiplied transgression,
    Chosen for myself my way.
Led by You to see my errors,
Lord, I tremble at Your terrors.

Yet, though conscience' voice appall me,
    Father, I will seek Your face;
Though Your child I dare not call me,
    Yet receive me in Your grace.
Do not for my sins forsake me;
Let Your wrath not overtake me.

For Your Son has suffered for me,
    Giv'n Himself to rescue me,
Died to save me and restore me,
    Reconciled and set me free.
Jesus' cross alone can vanquish
These dark fears and soothe this anguish.

Lord, on You I cast my burden—
    Sink it in the deepest sea!
Let me know Your gracious pardon,
    Cleanse me from iniquity.
Let Your Spirit leave me never;
Make me only Yours forever.

Lesson 7

Christ's Poverty, Our Wealth

Congregations know that if you want to raise the ire of church members, simply talk about money! When it comes to stewardship, one often hears, "All the church wants is my money." Whether or not Paul heard that excuse in his day, we really don't know. What we do know is that Christians need to help other Christians, and that this need was as great in Paul's day as it is now.

Acts 11 records a famine that impacted the Christians living in Jerusalem. Another factor that caused financial difficulties among early believers was persecution at the hands of Jewish religious leaders. Roman persecution would come later. Some Christians were ostracized and prevented from earning a living. So great was their need that believers in Antioch were encouraged "to send relief to the brothers living in Judea" (Acts 11:29).

The Christians in Judea lacked the funds for the barest of essentials, so they appealed to Paul and Barnabas for assistance. At first, the Corinthians had appeared eager to help their fellow believers. However, that changed when Paul departed for missionary work in Ephesus. As we will see, now that Paul was returning to Corinth, the Letter we know as 2 Corinthians would encourage them to complete the work that they had begun. Chapter 8 begins the second section of Paul's Letter, when he focuses on the current situation at Corinth.

The Grace of Giving

Some Christians believe that they are obligated to obey the Old Testament command concerning the tithe. Others maintain that they are completely free from any financial obligation whatsoever. Still others insist that God will reward them with financial wealth in return for their giving to Christ's Church. In contrast, Paul emphasizes the grace of giving.

75. Why do you suppose that the topic of giving to the Church is such a sensitive issue with so many Christians?

76. Why do you suppose that the topic of giving to the Church is so frequently misunderstood, even perhaps by you or members of your congregation?

Getting to the Heart of Stewardship

Three congregations comprised the Church in Macedonia: Berea, Thessalonica, and Philippi (Acts 16:11–17:14). The Philippians were well-known for their generosity toward Paul (Philippians 4:16). The Bereans also possessed the commendable attribute of confirming Paul's preaching and teaching with the words of Scripture (the Old Testament; Acts 17:11). Read 2 Corinthians 8:1–15.

77. What do we learn about the fledgling church in Thessalonica (1 Thessalonians 1:3)?

78. In spite of their extreme poverty (2 Corinthians 8:2), the Macedonian churches were wealthy in generosity (v. 2). To what radical extent did their desire to help the brethren in Judea extend (vv. 3–4)?

79. To whom did the Macedonians first give themselves (v. 5)? To whom, next (v. 5)? Ultimately, the Macedonians gave themselves to fellow believers in Judea. What do we learn from verse 5 about the source of Christian giving?

80. God's giving grace to us in Christ (8:1, 9) flows through us in our giving grace to others (vv. 6–7, 10–15). Might this "grace of giving," which is the heart of stewardship, inspire and enable believers to give . . . and to give generously?

A New Mission for Titus

During his conversation with Paul, Titus volunteered to return to Corinth to complete the task of collecting their offering.

Read 2 Corinthians 8:16–9:5.

81. You may recall from an earlier lesson that some Corinthians had labeled Paul untrustworthy. How does God use Titus and his two companions to counter this claim (8:20)?

82. How does this passage echo Hebrews 10:24–25? Who "stirred" the Macedonians into providing financial aid for the church in Jerusalem? By whose example are the churches in Achaia, of which the congregations in Corinth and Athens are part, "stirred on" in their giving?

The New Motivation behind Stewardship

In the Old Testament, God's people were commanded by the Law to tithe (Malachi 3:8–10). There is a new motivation for stewardship for the Christian.

Read 2 Corinthians 9:6–15.

83. In verse 5 of the previous section, Paul calls the Corinthians' contribution a "willing gift." Now, in verse 7, he writes that Christian giving should not be made "reluctantly" or "under compulsion." How does this contrast to the law of the Old Testament tithe?

84. The new motivation for the Christian is the fulfillment of His promises for us in Christ. What additional promises about giving does Paul remind the Corinthians of in verses 6 and 10?

God's Word for Today

Christians are no longer obligated to fulfill the Old Testament tithe (see Leviticus 27:30). However, they are inspired to give toward the Lord's work and to the care of the poor. God's rich grace to us in Christ, demonstrated in His extreme poverty, is the wellspring of Christian giving. Enabled by the Holy Spirit, cheerful hearts give generously.

85. What might we also learn about Christian giving from Jesus' discourse about the poor widow (Mark 12:41–44)?

86. Television "prosperity preachers" promise Christians that God will monetarily bless them, indeed handsomely, if Christians give to their "ministries." While God does indeed bless us through our giving, what is the proper understanding of this blessing (2 Corinthians 9:8–11)? Should Christians give in order to get?

In Closing

Encourage participants to begin the following activities:

- Discuss any change of heart you may have experienced after contemplating the difference between giving under obligation (because the Law says so or out of guilt) and giving cheerfully and from the heart (because of the Gospel).
- Comment on this statement: "The underlying factor in Christian giving is trust." How does that statement match the actions of the poor widow in our lesson?
- Read 2 Corinthians 10:1–18 to prepare for the next session.

Say or sing together the words of "O God, My Faithful God" (*LSB* 696; *LW* 371).

O God, my faithful God,
    True fountain ever flowing,
Without whom nothing is,
    All perfect gifts bestowing:
Give me a healthy frame,
    And may I have within
A conscience free from blame,
    A soul unstained by sin.

Grant me the strength to do
    With ready heart and willing
Whatever You command,
    My calling here fulfilling;
That I do what I should
    While trusting You to bless
The outcome for my good,
    For You must give success.

Keep me from saying words
   That later need recalling;
Guard me lest idle speech
   May from my lips be falling;
But when within my place
   I must and ought to speak,
Then to my words give grace
   Lest I offend the weak.

Lord, let me win my foes
   With kindly words and actions,
And let me find good friends
   For counsel and correction.
Help me, as You have taught,
   To love both great and small
And by Your Spirit's might
   To live in peace with all.

Let me depart this life
   Confiding in my Savior;
By grace receive my soul
   That it may live forever;
And let my body have
   A quiet resting place
Within a Christian grave;
   And let it sleep in peace.

And on that final day
   When all the dead are waking,
Stretch out Your mighty hand,
   My deathly slumber breaking.
Then let me hear Your voice,
   Redeem this earthly frame,
And bid me to rejoice
   With those who love Your name.

Lesson 8

Obedience to Christ

Chapter 10 begins the third and final section of Paul's Letter to the Corinthians. Having graced them with God's comfort, having shared with them his own hardships and fatherly care, having extolled the ministry of the new covenant, and having encouraged generous giving, Paul is now ready to prepare the congregation for his arrival.

In earlier chapters, Paul frequently used the plural pronoun *we* when addressing the Corinthians. That is about to change. Beginning with chapter 10, Paul takes a very frank, direct, and personal approach: he begins using the personal pronoun *I*. His mission is to rescue God's tender lambs from the hungry jaws of wolves known as the "super-apostles." A handful of subversives still existed within the Corinthian congregation, luring them away from God's Word. Satan is crafty, but Paul knows Satan is no match for God.

Paul's Spiritual Weapons

Paul is aware of the contrast between his manner of speaking and his manner of writing. In person, he appeared timid, reflecting the meekness of the Savior. Away, however, and in writing, Paul was very bold. He was especially bold in writing his earlier Letter (1 Corinthians), a boldness to which the Corinthians could attest.

Read 2 Corinthians 10:1–5.

87. Paul "appeals" and "begs" the congregation to come to their senses. With brotherly admonition, he appeals to their common faith in Christ, who was led "like a lamb . . . to the slaughter" (Isaiah 53:7). Why might Paul now use such an approach?

88. Paul had spoken to the Corinthians meekly once before. What was the context then (see 1 Corinthians 2:1–5)? Why would he have taken such an approach at that time?

89. The world wages war according to the flesh, that is, through power and coercion. Hence, Paul notes, "though we walk in the flesh, we are not waging war according to the flesh" (2 Corinthians 10:3). In what ways are spiritual battles different than physical battles?

90. In another Letter, Paul describes our spiritual weaponry much like a Roman soldier's weaponry (see Ephesians 6:11–20). All the weapons, save one, are defensive in nature. What is the lone offensive weapon in our spiritual arsenal?

The Power of the Gospel

The Word of God is "living and active" (Hebrews 4:12); it is "living and abiding" (1 Peter 1:23). The Gospel, God's Word of the forgiveness of our sins through Christ's cross, is God's power. Paul had reminded the Corinthians of this in his earlier Letter (1 Corinthians 1:18). And now in 2 Corinthians, when Paul speaks of "[destroying] arguments and every lofty opinion raised against the knowledge of God, and [taking] every thought captive to obey Christ" (2 Corinthians 10:5), he is addressing the power of the Gospel.

91. Paul contrasts the power of the Gospel with "arguments" and "every lofty opinion." Here he means human reason. What do you suppose is so unreasonable about the Gospel, from a merely human point of view?

92. When Paul wrote to the Corinthians the first time, he also contrasted the power of the Gospel with his own weakness, fear, and self-described inability (see 1 Corinthians 2:1–5). And yet, what was the result of Paul's preaching of the Gospel? Upon what does our faith rest (v. 5)?

Just as every modern congregation is comprised of different groups of people, so, too, was the congregation in Corinth. Paul notes that there are two groups he will deal with when he arrives at Corinth: the "super-apostles," who are undermining the Gospel and his work among the Corinthians; and those in the congregation who have been influenced by them. Read 2 Corinthians 10:6–11.

93. Which of these two groups will Paul deal with first (v. 6)? Why do you suppose that is?

94. Why is it important to differentiate between those who are weak in the faith and those who persist in false belief or practice? How might this look in Christian congregations today?

95. How will Paul demonstrate to his detractors, especially the "super-apostles," his boldness in person that he normally demonstrated only by letter (vv. 10–11)?

Paul's Ministry vs. the "Super-Apostles"

Paul had no need to compare himself to the "super-apostles." They judged their beliefs and actions by foolish standards: the ways of the world. In contrast, Paul wished to be judged by the standard set by

53

God: faithfulness to preaching and teaching the Gospel purely as commissioned by Christ. Read 2 Corinthians 10:12–18.

96. Paul did not enjoy boasting as did the "super-apostles" (see Galatians 6:14). Apparently, they thought of a mission field no further than Corinth. Ultimately, what does Paul hope to gain (2 Corinthians 10:15–16)?

97. In verse 17, Paul quotes the prophet Jeremiah (9:23–24). Why is boasting of one's accomplishments out-of-bounds for a servant of the Lord? What is the one thing that God requires of His servants (1 Corinthians 4:2)?

God's Word for Today

Paul was obedient to Christ. He relied on true spiritual weaponry against the vain reasoning and boasting of the "super-apostles." In Paul's weakness, he would proclaim the powerful Gospel. In Paul's strength, he would disarm, refute, and destroy the arguments and lofty opinions of his opponents.

98. Paul apparently was not a naturally gifted public speaker (2 Corinthians 10:10; see also 1 Corinthians 2:1). However, he relied on the power of God's Word, the power of the Gospel to change lives (2 Corinthians 2:2–5). How does the assurance of God's work in His Word give us comfort and enable us to tell others about Jesus?

99. Paul worked to make his thoughts obedient to Christ (2 Corinthians 10:5). While some may believe that Christianity is a "mindless" religion, how might Christians use their intellect in service to the Gospel?

In Closing

Encourage participants to begin the following activities:
- List the qualities that prove Paul to be an excellent role model for public ministry.
- Discuss how Paul is a prime example of the way outreach and nurturing walk hand in hand.
- Read 2 Corinthians 11:1–32 to prepare for the next session.

Speak or sing together the words of "Preserve Your Word, O Savior" (*LSB* 658:1–4; *LW* 337:1–4).

Preserve Your Word, O Savior,
    To us this latter day,
And let Your kingdom flourish;
    Enlarge Your Church, we pray.
O keep our faith from failing;
    Keep hope's bright star aglow.
Let nothing from truth turn us
    While living here below.

Preserve, O Lord, Your honor,
    The bold blasphemer smite;
Convince, convert, enlighten
    The souls in error's night.
Reveal Your will, dear Savior,
    To all who dwell below,
Great light of all the living,
    That all Your name may know.

Preserve, O Lord, Your Zion,
    Bought dearly with Your blood;
Protect what You have chosen
    Against the hellish flood.
Be always our defender
    When dangers gather round;
When all the earth is crumbling,
    Safe may Your Church be found.

Preserve Your Word and preaching,
    The truth that makes us whole,
The mirror of Your glory,
    The pow'r that saves the soul.
Oh, may this living water,
    This dew of heav'nly grace,
Sustain us while here living
    Until we see Your face.

Lesson 9

Different Spirit, Different Gospel

In the previous chapter, Paul resorted to the foolishness of boasting, but not about himself. In chapter 11, Paul will begin to hone in on the consequences of following the "super-apostles." This is far more than a "Paul said, they said" argument between two competing and equally valid truth claims. The debate here has eternal consequences.

Paul will systematically dissect many of the arguments used by the "super-apostles," who have tried to worm their way into the hearts of the Corinthians. Their gospel is false. And if the "super-apostles" have a different spirit and a different gospel, then listening to their message does not lead to salvation, but to damnation.

In the Garden of Eden, Satan tempted Eve by creating doubt in God's Word: "Did God *really* say . . . ?" (Genesis 3:1). The "super-apostles" are creating doubt in Paul's ministry and, ultimately, doubt in the true Gospel of Jesus Christ. Doubt has broken out and it spreads its pestilence with deadly results: "Is Paul *really* an apostle?"

Paul: Member of the Wedding Party

Now we come to one of the reasons Paul has been arguing so passionately and personally for the hearts and minds of the Corinthians. Like biblical imagery found elsewhere (see John 3:29–30; Ephesians 5:22–27; Revelation 19:7; 22:17), Paul describes God's people, the Church, as a bride. Read 2 Corinthians 11:1–2.

100. In John 3:29–30, John the Baptist describes himself as a

friend of the Bridegroom, Jesus. In 2 Corinthians 11:2, Paul describes himself as another important member of the wedding party. Who is it?

101. "Betrothed" to Christ in Baptism, Paul promised the Corinthians to their heavenly Bridegroom. In view of the "wedding" on the Last Day when He returns for His bride, what is Paul's concern?

Protecting Christ's Bride

Read 2 Corinthians 11:3–21. Ultimately, the source of the false teaching promoted by the "super-apostles" is Satan, who tempted Eve in the garden (v. 3).

102. How does Paul tie the true Jesus to the true Spirit and the true Gospel (v. 4)? Can we have the true Jesus if we believe false teachings about Him? Consider John 14:6 as you prepare your answer.

103. Paul confesses to not having the polished oratorical skills prized by the ancient Greeks. But what does Paul possess that is more important than oratorical skills (2 Corinthians 11:6)?

104. How does Paul defend himself from the charge that his teachings were of less value than those of the "super-apostles," who were trained public speakers, because unlike them he took no money from the Corinthians (vv. 7–9)?

105. What will Paul continue to do for the Corinthians (v. 12)? What damning charges does Paul bring against the "false apostles" (vv. 13–15)?

106. In verse 15, Paul mentions "righteousness," our right standing before God. Ultimately, what were the "super-apostles" proposing as a way of righteousness that was completely foreign to Paul's Gospel, the true Gospel of Jesus Christ?

Paul's Apostolic Suffering

Paul was a humble man who was not prone to boasting about his accomplishments. Instead, he boasted about his weaknesses. Faced with the possibility of seeing his spiritual daughter, the Corinthian congregation, defiled by the "super-apostles" before the return of her heavenly Bridegroom, Paul proves his love (see 11:11) by his suffering for the Gospel.

Read 2 Corinthians 11:22–30.

107. Jesus promised Paul that he would suffer for His sake (Acts 9:16). Recount Paul's suffering, which proves his loyalty to Christ and His Gospel.

108. Read 2 Corinthians 11:31–33. Paul humbly relates his embarrassing escape from Damascus (see Acts 9:23–25). How does this event—demonstrating Paul's weakness—show God's power in action (see 2 Corinthians 4:7)?

God's Word for Today

The "super-apostles" were of a different spirit. They proclaimed a different gospel. And, as such, they preached and taught a different Christ. As "father of the bride," Paul pointed to his weaknesses and sufferings as a sign of his fatherly love for the congregation in Corinth.

109. Are there false teachers today (Acts 20:29–31)? How do we identify them (Matthew 7:15–16; Acts 17:11; 2 Peter 2:1–3)?

110. Paul faithfully delivered the Gospel to the Corinthians (see 1 Corinthians 15:3–8). Take a few moments to compare this passage to the Apostles' Creed. How might the Creed be useful in conveying the Christian faith to someone who might not yet know Jesus?

In Closing

Encourage participants to begin the following activities:
- Review the importance of relating the Gospel message faithfully.
- Read 2 Corinthians 1:1–24 to prepare for the next session.

Sing or say together the words of "The Bridegroom Soon Will Call Us" (*LSB* 514; *LW* 176).

The Bridegroom soon will call us,
"Come to the wedding feast."
May slumber not befall us
Nor watchfulness decrease.
May all our lamps be burning
With oil enough and more
That we, with Him returning,
May find an open door!

There shall we see in glory
  Our dear Redeemer's face;
The long-awaited story
  Of heav'nly joy takes place:
The patriarchs shall meet us,
  The prophets' holy band;
Apostles, martyrs greet us
  In that celestial land.

There God shall from all evil
  Forever make us free,
From sin and from the devil,
  From all adversity,
From sickness, pain, and sadness,
  From troubles, cares, and fears,
And grant us heav'nly gladness
  And wipe away our tears.

In that fair home shall never
  Be silent music's voice;
With hearts and lips forever
  We shall in God rejoice,
While angel hosts are raising
  With saints from great to least
A mighty hymn for praising
  The Giver of the feast.

Lesson 10

Sufficient Grace

Although trials and tribulations were a part of Paul's life, he never felt as though God had turned His back on him. Paul's sufferings were a sign of his apostleship, and yet he never bragged about them to gain sympathy for himself. In our previous lesson, we noted that Paul "boasted" of his sufferings in 2 Corinthians 11:21–29. However, that boasting was to emphasize God's ability to work through his weaknesses.

Paul willingly suffered much to bring Christ's Gospel to a pagan world. He was the victim of numerous murder plots, endured trials before two Roman governors, had a trip to Rome short-circuited by a shipwreck, and suffered three years under house arrest, followed by a few years of freedom and a final arrest and imprisonment in the dreaded Mamertime dungeon. In AD 67 or 68, Paul met the executioner's axe on a road outside of Rome. God gave Paul a spirit (Romans 5:3–5) that was glorified in weakness.

Caught Up into Heaven

Apparently, in addition to their eloquent speaking abilities, the "super-apostles" were also boasting about their supposed religious experiences. Claims made by the "super-apostles" found sympathetic ears. Paul hesitantly and meekly responds by sharing with the Corinthians his heavenly experience that he describes only here and in no other place in the Bible.

Read 2 Corinthians 12:1–6.

111. Before his first missionary journey, Paul was "caught up" (see also 1 Thessalonians 4:17) bodily into paradise, or heaven. How

are believers strengthened by knowing what wonderful things are in store for them (see Romans 8:18)?

112. Although this incident happened years before, why did Paul wait until now to mention it? Why didn't he tell the Corinthians about his experience on his first visit (2 Corinthians 12:6)?

113. God does not promise every believer visions such as those He granted Paul. What other visions did Paul have (see Acts 16:9–10; 18:9–11)?

114. While the "super-apostles" bragged about their religious experiences, Paul was hesitant to even speak of his (2 Corinthians 12:6). What do you think Paul wanted the Corinthians to fully rely upon—extraordinary experiences or the Gospel?

God's Grace Is Sufficient

Now Paul quickly turns away from his experience in heaven to write again about his weaknesses. Here he mentions his "thorn in the flesh." While Paul never identifies this ailment specifically, Bible commentators have speculated that Paul suffered from any of a variety of persistent physical problems ranging from poor eyesight to a speech impediment to malaria. Whatever the painful condition or disease, the question of what Paul's "thorn in the flesh" was will remain unanswered this side of heaven.

Read 2 Corinthians 12:7–10.

115. Why did the Lord give Paul this "thorn"? What role did Satan play in this?

116. At first, Paul didn't recognize the reason why he had this "thorn" (v. 8). Why did God allow the "thorn" to remain?

117. Read Matthew 5:1–12; 26:36–46. Should we expect suffering in our lives as Christians? How do these verses contrast with some Christian teachers today who suggest otherwise?

118. Ultimately, Paul surrendered to the Lord's will that he suffer. In faith, Paul recognized that God had answered no to his prayer to remove the thorn. Where did Paul find strength to accept the Lord's answer (2 Corinthians 12:9; see also 2 Timothy 1:18)?

119. Relying on the Lord's grace in Christ, Paul was able to accept other weaknesses and hardships in his life as well (2 Corinthians 12:10). Take some time now to share how God has strengthened and deepened your faith in the midst of your sufferings.

Paul Anticipates His Return to Corinth

Paul is now ready to discuss his upcoming visit to Corinth. He reinforces what he wrote earlier—that he does not want to be a financial burden upon them. He has acted honestly in making financial requests of them through Titus; although he has received good word from Titus about the congregation (2 Corinthians 7:16), he continues to worry that they may fall back into their old ways.

Read 2 Corinthians 12:11–21.

120. Jesus promised His apostles special gifts that would accompany their Gospel ministries (see Mark 16:14–20; Luke 9:1–2). What were these gifts given to Paul (2 Corinthians 12:12; see also Romans 15:18–19)?

121. Paul expresses his concern that he still may find impenitence in the Corinthian congregation, which God will use to humble him (2 Corinthians 12:20–21). What might be the positive result of such humbling in Paul and in pastors today?

God's Word for Today

Like Paul, because we follow our suffering Savior, we can expect hardships and difficulties in our lives as Christians. We call upon our gracious God in prayer; however, sometimes His answer is no. In our weaknesses, God manifests His sufficient grace for us, because His "power is made perfect in weakness" (2 Corinthians 12:9).

122. Review 2 Corinthians 1:3–6; see also Psalm 50:15. In spite of our own sufferings, God gives us the strength to comfort others in the midst of their suffering. Discuss some ways that you can provide assistance to those who experience hardships in your congregation.

In Closing

Encourage participants to begin the following activities:
- Review Martin Luther's Small Catechism for Luther's explanation of the Third Petition of the Lord's Prayer.
- Describe what might have been an ideal environment for Paul to have found upon his third visit to Corinth.
- Read 2 Corinthians 13:1–14 to prepare for the next session.

Say or sing together the words of "If God Himself Be for Me" (*LSB* 724:1, 2, 3, 6; *LW* 407:1, 2, 3, 6).

If God Himself be for me,
    I may a host defy;
For when I pray, before me
    My foes, confounded, fly.
If Christ, my head and master,
    Befriend me from above,
What foe or what disaster
    Can drive me from His love?

I build on this foundation,
    That Jesus and His blood
Alone are my salvation,
    My true, eternal good.
Without Him all that pleases
    Is valueless on earth;
The gifts I have from Jesus
    Alone have priceless worth.

Christ Jesus is my splendor,
    My sun, my light, alone;
Were He not my defender
    Before God's judgment throne,
I never should find favor
    And mercy in His sight,
But be destroyed forever
    As darkness by the light.

Who clings with resolution
  To Him whom Satan hates
Must look for persecution;
  For him the burden waits
Of mock'ry, shame, and losses
  Heaped on his blameless head;
A thousand plagues and crosses
  Will be his daily bread.

Next Class
6/14/19

Lesson 11

The God of Love and Peace

In *Evangelism in the Early Church* (Hodder and Stoughton, London, 1970), Michael Green notes that the Roman Empire recognized only two religions: *religio*, the official state religion, and *superstitio*, the private faith of individuals. *Superstitio* were tolerated by the Romans so long as they did not compete directly against the Roman polytheistic cult. Rome exercised "tolerance" with private beliefs practiced at home so long as citizens supported the public worship of the pagan gods. Only the Jews were excluded from this demand for public worship because of their unswerving, monotheistic faith.

In some parts of the Roman Empire, Christians would suffer for their faith, paying even with their lives. Like Peter and all the other apostles, save for John, Paul would give his life for his Lord. Resolute and unwavering in his faith, he had been called to serve Jesus, his Savior, who through the weakness of His cross had restored Paul and all of us to the God of love and peace.

A New Call to Repentance

As we enter the final chapter of 2 Corinthians, Paul tenders issues he wants resolved before his arrival. Paul obviously was bold and confrontational during his "painful visit." Righteous anger brought on by the thought of the Corinthians losing their souls for eternity fueled his zeal.

Read 2 Corinthians 13:1–10.

123. Paul notes that "every charge must be established by the evidence of two or three witnesses" (v. 1; see also Deuteronomy 19:15

68

and Matthew 18:15–19). Why do you think it is important, especially in the Church, to be diligent in restoring sinners patiently and fairly?

124. Some modern legal documents, including marriage licenses, are required to have at least two witnesses. What are the obvious benefits to such a practice?

125. What two groups does Paul want specifically addressed? What matters does Paul want settled before his arrival (v. 2)?

126. In what ways do Paul's life and ministry mirror Christ's (vv. 3b–4)?

127. How will the Corinthians know that Paul's apostolic ministry is genuine (vv. 5–7)?

Fishing was a common trade during ancient times, and Paul borrows a fishing term to drive home an important point in verse 9. The term is *restoration*, and it was the word used for the mending of torn nets (Mark 1:19). This word has since come to mean restoring a Christian to the path of salvation (Galatians 6:1).

128. With the above definition in mind, what message is Paul conveying to the Corinthians?

129. Ultimately, what is Paul's goal for his forthcoming visit (2 Corinthians 13:10)? How does this reflect what Paul wrote them earlier about his Gospel ministry to them (see 1:18–20; 2:17; 3:6–11; 5:18–20; 6:1–2)?

Paul's Closing and Trinitarian Benediction

Having made his brotherly appeal, Paul is now ready to conclude his Letter. He offers four final admonitions and writes his final words in the form of a benediction, a blessing invoking our triune God: Father, Son, and Holy Spirit.

Read 2 Corinthians 13:11–14.

130. Although Paul had sometimes used harsh words in his dealings with the Corinthians, he dearly loves them and recognizes them as fellow Christians. How do we especially note this in verse 11?

131. Paul encourages the congregation to be "restored" to God in Christ, to pay close attention to what he has written them ("listen to my appeal"), and to avoid a party spirit ("agree with one another," and "live in peace" [v. 11]). How were these admonitions especially appropriate for the Corinthians?

132. Although Paul is miles away in Macedonia, he desires that the Corinthians know that they are not alone in their faith. What evidence do you find that conveys Paul's desire?

133. 2 Corinthians is the only Letter Paul wrote that ends with a trinitarian benediction (13:14). Notice how all three persons of the Godhead are mentioned: Father, Son, and Holy Spirit. What does Paul desire for the Corinthians above all else?

God's Word for Today

The Bible does not tell us the results of Paul's Letter or his latter visit to the Corinthians. However, the Bible does tell us that on his third visit Paul spent three months in Corinth (Acts 20:3). During this stay, Paul wrote to the church in Rome and told them that he would travel on to Spain at the conclusion of his visit in Corinth (Romans 15:23–29).

134. "Grace . . . love . . . and fellowship" (2 Corinthians 13:14) are divine gifts given by our gracious God. What examples of these three gifts have you experienced in your congregation? How else might these gifts be shared with those in your community who do not yet know God's sufficient grace?

In Closing

Sing or speak together the words of "I Trust, O Christ, in You Alone" (*Lutheran Service Builder/LSB Accompaniment Edition* 972; *LW* 357).

I trust, O Christ, in You alone;
    No earthly hope avails me.
You will not see me overthrown
    When Satan's host assails me.
No human strength, no earthly pow'r
Can see me through the evil hour,
    For You alone my strength renew.
    I cry to You!
    I trust, O Lord, Your promise true.

My sin and guilt are plaguing me;
    O grant me true contrition
And by Your death upon the tree
    Your pardon and remission.
Before the Father's throne above
Recall Your matchless deed of love
    That He may lift my dreadful load,
    O Son of God!
    I plead the grace Your death bestowed.

Confirm in us Your Gospel, Lord,
    Your promise of salvation.
And make us keen to hear Your Word
    And follow our vocation:
To spend our lives in love for You
To bear each other's burdens too.
    And then, at last, when death shall loom,
    O Savior, come
    And bear Your loved ones safely home.

Leader Notes

Preparing to Teach 2 Corinthians

To prepare to lead this study, read through the Book of 2 Corinthians. For background on the many multifaceted problems facing the early Christian church that Paul established in Corinth, you may also want to read 1 Corinthians. You might secure a good commentary on both books and read them over or read the introduction to the books in the *Concordia Self-Study Bible* or a Bible handbook. A reading of Acts 9:1–31, detailing Paul's conversion, would also be helpful as background, as would several maps showing Paul's missionary journeys in the first century AD.

These notes are provided as a "safety net," a place to turn for help in answering questions and for enriching discussion. It will not answer every question raised in your class. Please read it, along with the questions, before class. Consult it in class only after exploring the Bible references and discussing what they teach. Please note the different abilities of your class members. Some will easily find the Bible passages listed in this study; others will struggle. To make participation easier, team up members of the class. For example, if a question asks you to look up several passages, assign one passage to one group, the second to another, and so on. Divide the work! Let participants present the answers they discover.

The materials in these notes are designed to help you in leading others through this portion of the Holy Scriptures. Nevertheless, this booklet is to be an aid to and not a substitute for your own study of and preparation for teaching the Book of 2 Corinthians.

If you have the opportunity, you will find it helpful to make use of other biblical reference works in the course of your study. These commentaries can be very helpful: David J. Valleskey, *Second Corinthians*, People's Bible Commentary Series (Milwaukee: Northwestern Publishing House, 1992; reprinted by Concordia Publishing House, 2005); Colin Kruse, *2 Corinthians*, Tyndale New Testament Commentaries (Grand Rapids, MI: Eerdmans, 1991); and Philip E. Hughes, *The Second Epistle to the Corinthians*, The New

International Commentary on the New Testament (Grand Rapids, MI: Eerdmans, 1992). Although it is not strictly a commentary, the section on 2 Corinthians in *The Word Becoming Flesh* by Horace Hummel (St. Louis: Concordia Publishing House, 1970) also contains valuable material for the proper interpretation of this biblical book.

Group Bible Study

Group Bible study means mutual learning from one another under the guidance of a leader. The Bible is an inexhaustible resource. No one person can discover all it has to offer. In a class, many eyes see many things and can apply them to many life situations. As the leader, you should resist the temptation to "give the answers" and so act as an authority. This teaching approach stifles participation by individual members and can actually hamper learning. As a general rule, the teacher is not to *give* interpretation but to *develop* interpreters. Of course, there are times when you should and must share insights and information gained by your study of the lesson. And you'll want to engage class members in meaningful sharing and discussion of all points, leading them to a summary of the lesson at the close. As a general rule, don't explain what the learners can discover by themselves.

Have a chalkboard and chalk or newsprint and marker available to emphasize significant points of the lesson. Rephrase your inquiries or the inquiries of participants as questions, problems, or issues. This provokes thought. Keep discussion to the point. List on the chalkboard or newsprint the answers given. Then determine the most vital points made in the discussion. Ask additional questions to fill gaps.

The aim of every Bible study is to help people grow spiritually, not merely in biblical and theological knowledge, but in Christian thinking and living. This means growth in Christian attitudes, insights, and skills for Christian living. The focus of this course must be the Church and the world of our day. The guiding question will be this: What does the Lord teach us for life today through the apostle Paul?

Pace Your Teaching

The lessons in this course of study are designed for a study session of at least an hour in length. If it is the desire and intent of the class to complete an entire lesson each session, it will be necessary for you to summarize the content of certain answers or biblical references in order to preserve time. Asking various class members to look up different Bible passages and to read them aloud to the rest of the class will save time over having every class member look up each reference.

Also, you may not want to cover every question in each lesson. Doing so could lead to undue haste and frustration. Be selective. Pace your teaching. Spend no more than five to ten minutes opening the lesson. During the lesson, get the sweep of meaning. Occasionally stop to help the class gain understanding of a word or concept. Allow approximately five minutes for closing the lesson and announcements.

Should your group have more than a one-hour class period, you can be more leisurely, but do not allow any lesson to drag and become tiresome. Keep it moving. Keep it alive. Keep it meaningful. Eliminate some questions and restrict yourself to those questions most meaningful to the members of the class. If most members study the text at home, they can report their findings, and the time gained can be applied to relating the lesson to life.

Good Preparation

Good preparation by you, the leader, usually affects the pleasure and satisfaction the class will experience.

Suggestions to the Leader for Using the Study Guide

The Lesson Pattern

This set of lessons is designed to aid *Bible study*, that is, to aid a consideration of the written Word of God, with discussion and personal application growing out of the text at hand.

The typical lesson is divided into these sections:
1. Theme Verse
2. Objectives
3. Questions and Answers
4. Closing

The theme verse and objectives give you assistance in arousing the interest of the group in the concepts of the lesson. Here is where you stimulate the minds of the class members. Do not linger too long over the introductory remarks.

The questions and answers provide the real spadework necessary for Bible study. Here the class digs, uncovers, and discovers; it gets the facts and observes them. Your comments are needed only to the extent that they help the group understand the text. The questions in this guide, corresponding to sections within the text, are intended to help the participants discover the meaning of the text.

Having determined what the text says, the class is ready to apply the message. Having heard, read, marked, and learned the Word of God, proceed to digest it inwardly through discussion, evaluation, and application. This is done, as this guide suggests, by taking the truths found in Scripture and applying them to the world and Christianity in general and then to personal Christian life. Class time may not permit discussion of all questions and topics. In preparation, you may need to select one or two and focus on them. Close the session by reviewing one important truth from the lesson.

Remember, the Word of God is sacred, but this study guide is not. The notes in this section offer only guidelines and suggestions. Do not hesitate to alter the guidelines or substitute others to meet your needs and the needs of the participants. Adapt your teaching plan to your class and your class period. Good teaching directs the learner to discover for himself or herself. For you, the teacher, this means directing the learner, not giving the learner answers. Choose the verses that should be looked up in Scripture. What discussion questions will you ask? At what points? Write them in the margin of your study guide. Involve class members, but give them clear directions. What practical actions might you propose for the week following the lesson? Which of the items do you consider most important for your class?

How will you best use your teaching period? Do you have forty-five minutes? an hour? or an hour and a half? If time is short, what should you cut? Learn to become a wise steward of class time.

Be sure to take time to summarize the lesson, or have a class member do it. Plan a brief opening devotion, using members of the class.

Remember to pray frequently for yourself and your class. May God the Holy Spirit bless your study and your leading of others into the comforting truths of God's Christ-centered Word.

Lesson 1

The God of All Comfort

Theme verse: *Blessed be the God and Father of our Lord Jesus Christ, the Father of mercies and God of all comfort.*

2 Corinthians 1:3

Objectives

By the power of the Holy Spirit working through God's Word, we will

- learn the historic background of the people and city of Corinth prior to Paul's missionary visit;
- discover the conflicts Paul faces within the Corinthian church;
- witness how God has comforted Paul in his times of trial and tribulation;
- watch as Paul offers this same comfort to the Corinthians in the midst of their struggles.

Setting the Stage

1. Ongoing problems in the congregation included internal bickering over whom to follow: Paul, Apollos, Cephas, or Christ (1 Corinthians 1:11–12). When Paul left Corinth to work in Ephesus, his position was taken by others and conflicts arose over the importance of each pastor. Another conflict arose over disbelief that Christ rose from the dead (1 Corinthians 15:16). The Greeks found it impossible to believe that the dead will rise again.

2. Some members of the Corinthian church found it difficult to separate themselves from their former lives of debauchery. Paul called them to disassociate themselves from their former behavior and those still engaged in such practices (1 Corinthians 5:9–11). He also chided them for taking frivolous lawsuits against fellow believers into court

(1 Corinthians 6:1). Another argument within the Corinthian church centered on whether or not food offered to idols could be eaten (1 Corinthians 8:4).

Paul's Third Letter

3. The writer is identified as Paul, an apostle of Jesus Christ, by the will of God. Timothy is identified as someone with Paul as he writes his Letter, which is addressed to the church at Corinth and the saints in Achaia, which includes Corinth. If available, locate Achaia on a map of the region. It was common for letters of Paul's day to circulate among the congregations of a region. 2 Corinthians is no exception.

4. Paul acts on the authority that he received from Jesus Christ as an apostle (one "sent forth"). We might call such a person an envoy, someone who represents another. In Paul's case, his authority was derived from Jesus Christ's direct and immediate calling of him to the Office of Holy Ministry.

5. Paul's desire was that God's grace would fill the hearts of the Corinthians and bring them the peace with God they so desperately needed in their time of conflict. Because this Letter bears apostolic authority and was written under the inspiration of the Holy Spirit, Paul's blessing is no mere pious sentiment. His words convey what they say.

God's Comfort

6. Normally Paul begins his Letters with a word of thanksgiving, but 2 Corinthians offers an exception. Conflicts have caused a split within the Corinthian congregation and, instead of a word of thanksgiving, Paul asks God to bring comfort through his words as their spiritual father and pastor.

7. Paul uses the words *comfort* or *comforted* some ten times in these verses. These tend to highlight the need Paul perceives among the Corinthians. In his first Letter, he was rather direct; in his second, he will be comforting.

8. Paul shows that God comforted him during times when he faced a death sentence, and delivered him through this peril (vv. 9–10). Because God's hand has protected Paul, he assures them that God will see the Corinthians through their time of conflict. Paul testifies that he takes great comfort in God's protection and so should they. Paul

mentions that God raised Christ from the dead to make the point that nothing is impossible for God. If God can raise Christ from the dead, surely He can resolve any struggles the Corinthians are facing.

These words offer assurances to you and me in our times of personal struggles. As we explore 2 Corinthians further, we will learn that a death sentence was but one of many crises Paul faced in his life (see 11:23–28). In each situation, God protected Paul and worked through him to achieve His purposes. Those who read 2 Corinthians can take comfort in Paul's testimony of God's faithfulness and provision.

9. Verse 11 associates Paul's very survival with the prayers of others. In no way should we diminish the importance of our prayers for others or the prayers that other believers make on our behalf. God graciously promises to hear and answer our prayers made in faith in Christ and made in accordance with His will.

God's Word for Today

10. Answers will vary. Allow participants to discuss those persons or institutions that provided help when they needed it. Participants should ponder how they themselves might provide comfort to others at home, in their congregation, at work, in school, and so on.

11. God knows our limitations and always provides a "way of escape" for us. Assist participants in discussing their own experiences in this regard. Sometimes we will recall a Bible verse that helps us in temptation; sometimes we'll recall promises that we have made. In any case, when we are tempted, we call out to our heavenly Father in prayer, saying, as the Lord taught us, "deliver us from evil."

12. Answers will vary. Assist participants in discussing those times in which they experienced trials and tribulations, but nevertheless learned (perhaps only years later) that God worked all things for their good.

Lesson 2

God's Answer Is Yes!

Theme verse: *For all the promises of God find their Yes in Him (Christ).*

2 Corinthians 1:20

Objectives

By the power of the Holy Spirit working through God's Word, we will

- discover Paul's acknowledgement that he has preached faithfully;
- learn why Paul changed his plans to visit Corinth;
- watch as Paul defends himself from charges brought against his ministry;
- learn the value of preaching both Law and Gospel.

First Charge: Paul Is Hard to Understand

13. Some Corinthians accused Paul of delivering messages that were difficult to understand. However, the simple truth that Paul preached and taught consistently was this: Christ redeemed us with His blood and has made us heirs of the kingdom of God.

14. Paul desires that on the Last Day the Corinthians can "boast" in (take pride in) the salvation that God has shown them through Paul's ministry, and that Paul can "boast" in the salvation the Holy Spirit has worked for the Corinthians through him. There is always room for Christians to grow in their faith (1 Peter 2:2). It is Paul's desire that on the Last Day the Corinthians can point with pride to Paul as a symbol of God's faithfulness, just as Paul desires to point to the Corinthians with pride in what God has done. Paul expressed these same feelings for the Thessalonians (1 Thessalonians 2:19–20).

80

Second Charge: Paul Is Untrustworthy

15. Answers will vary. Accusations of untrustworthiness strike deeply, causing anger and hurt and sometimes even germinating thoughts of revenge.

16. Paul originally planned to travel directly from Ephesus to Corinth, then head north into Macedonia to visit the churches there. He would then travel back to Corinth before heading to Judea. The result would be a double visit to Corinth. By God's call, Paul deviated from his original travel plans. As we learn in 2 Corinthians 2:1, Paul had made a "painful visit" to Corinth previous to this one. It seems God was pleased to allow His Word to work through the Corinthian church before Paul visited again.

17. We gather that Paul was more concerned that the Corinthians believe the Gospel message than his explanation of his travel plans. Nevertheless, Paul called on God as his witness to testify to the validity of why he changed his itinerary.

18. Two of God's promises lead us to the truth in God's Word. First, God promised Adam and Eve a Savior, a Victor over Satan (Genesis 3:15). Second, God promised Abram that "all the families of the earth shall be blessed" through his Seed, namely Christ (Genesis 12:3, 7; 13:15; 24:7). These promises, and many others, find their fulfillment, their Yes!, in Jesus Christ. The Holy Spirit, through the Yes! of Christ, allowed the Corinthians to remain in their faith (2 Corinthians 1:22; Ephesians 1:13; 4:30).

Third Charge: Paul Is Too Harsh

19. Here we find Paul's reasoning. It was too soon after his "painful visit" to travel directly to Corinth. Paul wanted a joyful third visit and apparently the Holy Spirit was still working the repentance needed to make that possible.

20. The words in 1 Corinthians appear harsh at first blush, for the Corinthians were to remove from their midst a man engaged in an incestuous relationship with his stepmother. With Paul's concerns in mind, excommunication is not a harsh response. The purpose of excommunication is to maintain purity within a congregation, as well as to bring the excommunicated sinner to repentance, restoring him or her to Christ and His Church.

21. Satan desires to outwit us and lead us into hell. An application of the Law is needed to bring the sinner face-to-face with his or her sin

so that with a contrite heart he or she can sorrowfully grieve over his or her actions against God. The Gospel brings relief and the forgiveness of sin. It also restores the sinner's relationship with God and people, outwitting Satan in the process (2 Corinthians 2:8–11). If we are not careful in applying both Law and Gospel, contrite sinners may be led to despair while unrepentant sinners may be led into further sin.

God's Word for Today

22. Paul's actions support the application of the Law first, followed by the application of the Gospel. Paul seeks excommunication (Law) for the sinner (1 Corinthians 5:5). Obviously, by the time Paul wrote 2 Corinthians, excommunication has worked repentance, for Paul asks the Corinthians to forgive the guilty party and restore him to their congregation (2 Corinthians 2:5–11).

23. Ultimately, the purpose of excommunication is the salvation of souls. Excommunication provides a separation designed to prevent the spread of sin within a congregation. In addition, it signifies to the sinner the seriousness of violating God's Law so that, seeing the error of his or her ways, he or she might repent and return to communion with God. Excommunication should not be something the Church takes lightly or administers indiscriminately. It must be executed wisely for the salvation of souls, which is God's highest priority (1 Timothy 2:3–4).

24. Christ commands that we rebuke our brother or sister who sins in order that he or she may repent. When he or she does, we are to forgive him or her. Notice also that Christ commands forgiveness *each time* the sinner repents. In Paul we see this exemplified, as he rebukes and then freely forgives the penitent sinner.

Lesson 3

Superiority of the New Covenant

Theme verse: *Now the Lord is the Spirit, and where the Spirit of the Lord is, there is freedom.*

2 Corinthians 3:17

Objectives

By the power of the Holy Spirit working through God's Word, we will

- discover the assurance Paul has of Christ's triumphal victory;
- witness how the Corinthians are Paul's "letter from Christ";
- gain an understanding of the Holy Spirit's role in helping Paul;
- receive insight into the "false apostles" who would derail Paul's missionary work in Corinth.

Paul in Macedonia

25. Paul did not want to cause the Corinthians additional pain until he had learned if his earlier words had brought about the desired "obedience." He was hoping that Titus's presence might bring him some peace of mind.

26. Answers will vary. Most people can identify with having to speak the truth either to one's children, employees, friends, or neighbors, and experiencing the sleepless night or nights that follow.

The New Covenant's Superiority

27. The victorious general is Jesus; Satan and his evil hordes are the vanquished.

28. In Martin Luther's hymn of the Reformation, based on Psalm 46, we again are presented the image of the victorious Christ and the vanquished Satan. Luther's symbolism of how Jesus' "one little word" subdues Satan offers Christians great hope, as does Paul's description of a Roman "triumph." Speculation abounds as to what "little word" Luther was thinking of; perhaps it was Jesus' word from the cross: *tetelestai*, "It is finished" (John 19:30).

29. We learn here that some workers among the Corinthians were "preaching" the Gospel to them in exchange for money. Receiving payment for publicly teaching philosophy was common during this time. However, Paul never took money while he was among the Corinthians. As we will learn in a later lesson, Paul's missionary work in Corinth was financed by the Macedonian churches.

30. Metaphorically speaking, because of the Spirit's work through the Gospel in the lives of the Corinthians, they were like letters of testimony affirming Paul's ministry. In a similar way, you and I are like letters affirming the ministry of our pastor(s) and teachers.

31. Just as Paul did many centuries before him, Martin Luther knew that he possessed no powers or abilities of his own to convert those around him to faith in Christ. The gifts these men possessed came only by the power of God through the Holy Spirit. They were merely conduits the Lord was using to pour His blessings into the lives of others.

32. a. Law; b. Gospel; c. Law; d. Gospel; e. Law; f. Gospel; g. Law; h. Gospel; i. Law; j. Gospel; k. Law; l. Gospel.

33. Allow participants to discuss the many ways Satan "veils," or attempts to hide, the Gospel: he twists God's Word through false doctrine, he influences false teachers, he tempts us to sin, he tempts us to minimalize sin in our lives or in the lives of others, he tempts us to take our eyes off of Jesus and to focus on our own righteousness, and so on.

God's Word for Today

34. As hearers of the Gospel, in faith we are enabled by the Spirit to respect and to love our Gospel preachers and teachers, and to obey them in matters dictated by Holy Scripture.

35. Answers will vary. Guide participants in applying the biblical truth that the light that we shine upon others is actually Christ's light shining within us. What does that look like at home? At school? At work? In the parish? In the community?

36. The world and all its enticements, and even the old covenant, pales in comparison with the new covenant in Christ Jesus. In Him, our sins have been atoned for. Through Him, we have been restored to a right relationship with God our heavenly Father. By Him, we have the presence of the Holy Spirit, who dwells in our hearts as His temple. Truly, nothing is as grand and glorious as the glory of the new life we have in Jesus Christ.

Lesson 4

Treasure in Clay Jars

Theme verse: *We have this treasure in jars of clay, to show that the surpassing power belongs to God and not to us.*

2 Corinthians 4:7

Objectives

By the power of the Holy Spirit working through God's Word, we will
- learn about Paul's *jars of clay* metaphor;
- understand Paul's *tent* metaphor;
- grow in our comprehension of the glory of eternal life;
- discover God's call to "walk by faith."

The Potter and the Clay

37. Answers will vary. Guide participants in discussing both the joys and frustrations of artistry.

38. After firing, glazing, and firing again, clay becomes functional, but it is not unbreakable.

Paul's *Jars of Clay* Metaphor

39. The word *but* indicates a new contrast ahead in Paul's thoughts. Paul contrasts the glory of the new covenant with the fragile human vessels carrying that message . . . "the jars of clay."

40. God shapes the messenger for useful service. Those who are familiar with working with clay will be able to attest to the mixing, the pulling, the rolling, the throwing, and all the other activities that must be done *to* the clay in order to make it useful. In the same way, God

86

must work *upon us* through trials and tribulations in order to form us into the desired shape He has planned for us.

41. We learn in our text that Paul has been "afflicted," "perplexed," and "struck down," leaving us with an image of human clay molded and shaped by the Master Potter. Interestingly, Genesis 2 describes God forming man in much the same way as a potter would form a clay vessel. In 2:7, the Hebrew word for "form" is used to describe a potter's work with clay (see Isaiah 45:9; Jeremiah 18:6). Also, "man" in Hebrew is much like the Hebrew word for "ground"; man is formed from the "dust" of the ground, or a dry earth element, as is clay; and God breathed into man's nostrils the breath of life—and breath, as we know, contains moisture. Thus, we are indeed God's human clay vessels, to be molded and shaped by Him.

42. John the Baptist understood the superiority of Christ. He could call the masses to repent and to be baptized for the forgiveness of sins, but only Christ had the power in Himself to forgive. Likewise, Paul realized that we are not the power behind Christ's message of salvation—God is. This message should provide comfort to us as Christ's Church, for the effectiveness of God's Word does not depend on how well we deliver that message. God's Word is efficacious on its own and receives no power from the messenger.

43. In his first Letter to Timothy, Paul writes that God desires the salvation of everyone and that salvation comes only though their belief in Jesus Christ. Through the apostle Paul, Christ's chosen, weak vessel of clay, God would work out His gracious will.

Paul's Heavenly Dwelling

44. During his first mission trip to Corinth, Paul plied his trade as a tentmaker in order to support himself. A tent is a particularly apt metaphor, or object lesson, for Paul to use in writing to the Corinthians, since they were aware of this, his other vocational ability.

45. A tent is a temporary dwelling and therefore subject to the destructive forces of the elements. Although sturdy, it will not last forever. Jars of clay, while useful and sturdily made for their purposes, also will not last forever.

46. Paul longs for his "heavenly dwelling," that is, his resurrected body free from suffering and pain. As long as we live upon this earth, our bodies become weaker and more fragile, just as tents begin to decompose over time and jars of clay become more subject to being broken. Nevertheless, the gracious Lord is with us, whether here in this

earthly body or there in our resurrected bodies. Knowing this inspires our confidence in Him who holds us in His gracious hand, body and soul.

God's Word for Today

47. Paul understands that he has no merits or abilities apart from what God has granted him in Christ. He trusts God with his whole heart to provide and care for him, not worrying about what tomorrow will bring. Paul's life is a joyful response to the Gospel of Christ. Such a living faith does not cause us to remain in sorrow or doubt, but strengthens us with a joy that cannot be taken away.

48. Everyone will be held accountable for his actions by God on the Last Day. Christians will be rewarded for good works done in response to the Gospel, not because of any obligations imposed by the Law. Their sins are covered by the blood of Christ. Unbelievers, because they lacked faith, will have no good works. They will be punished for their sins. Paul was absolutely confident that "Christ will be honored in [his] body, whether by life or by death" (Philippians 1:20). Christians have the same confidence, for we are saved by God's grace through faith in Jesus Christ.

Lesson 5

Ministry of Reconciliation

Theme verse: *All this is from God, who through Christ reconciled us to Himself and gave us the ministry of reconciliation.*

2 Corinthians 5:18

Objectives

By the power of the Holy Spirit working through God's Word, we will

- discover Paul's defense against those who would attack his apostolic integrity;
- contemplate Paul's ministry of reconciliation;
- grow in our understanding of what it means to be "unequally yoked";
- rejoice in our roles as Christ's ambassadors.

Another Charge against Paul

49. Allow participants to review this passage, discussed in the previous lesson under question 48. Paul is unafraid of the verdict God will render about his ministry. While Paul certainly made mistakes, as we all do, Paul was unafraid of the final verdict that God will render because of God's tremendous grace in Christ.

50. Paul was trying to "persuade" others so that they might be won for Christ through his ministry among the Corinthians.

Paul's Defense

51. "For the love of Christ," Paul was willing to endure all manner of hardships. Christ's love of Paul was not dependant on Paul's works. Christ's love is unconditional. Paul was responding to that love

by extending salvation to others that they, too, might be reconciled to God through Christ.

52. No, Paul was not concerned about how others perceived him, for Paul was "known to God" (5:11b). Paul's chief concern was that the Corinthians learn of God's reconciliation through Christ.

53. Paul no longer allows the way of the world, the way of the flesh, to influence the way that he sees others. Formerly, in his old way of life, that was how he also viewed Jesus.

54. Paul's defense was that he was an ambassador for Christ and that he brought God's message: through Jesus Christ, God has reconciled sinful people to Himself.

Paul's Ministry of Reconciliation

55. Paul calls himself an "ambassador" for Christ (v. 20). An ambassador is someone who "speaks on behalf of" or "represents" someone. Paul does not represent himself in these important matters of salvation. As a called minister of the Gospel, he represented Jesus. Someone might receive Christ's message of salvation in vain by hearing it and afterwards ignoring it.

56. Paul was very concerned that he live an exemplary life before the Corinthians (v. 3). He did not point to the increases in worship attendance, the number of conversions, the square footage of new buildings, or the wonderful programs he had initiated among them, but rather to the tremendous sufferings he had undergone for the sake of the Gospel. What a marvelous counter-claim to the false accusations of the "super-apostles," as we shall see later in 2 Corinthians and, sadly, to the fleshly boastings of some contemporary churches and ministers.

57. Paul opens himself up completely to the Corinthians (vv. 11–12). His transparency and sensitivity toward them are the work of the Holy Spirit through the Gospel. He is their spiritual father, just as they are his spiritual children (v. 13).

Unequal Yoking

58. False teachings are like poison—they make us spiritually sick and have the potential to kill us. Like the Bereans (Acts 17:11), we should study the Scriptures to see if what we're hearing from the sanctuary pulpit and the classroom lectern conforms to the Word of God. There is no fellowship between Christ and darkness. We should avoid false teachers (Romans 16:17). While we will come into contact

with unbelievers in our daily life and work, we should not participate in the prayer and worship of false gods.

59. Paul clearly teaches that believers should only marry other believers ("in the Lord"). If unbelievers and believers are already married, they should remain married, because the unbelieving partner may come to faith through the believing partner (1 Corinthians 7:12–16).

God's Word for Today

60. *Reconciliation* is essentially restoring a good relationship. Our sinful nature separates us from God, but the atoning sacrifice of Jesus Christ on Calvary's cross restored our good relationship with God. It is important for believers to realize they did nothing to effect or to merit this reconciliation. Reconciliation is a gift of grace from a loving God. Likewise, because "in Christ God was reconciling the world to Himself, not counting their trespasses against them, and entrusting to us the message of reconciliation" (2 Corinthians 5:19), we can be about reconciling people to God, and persons to other persons, through sharing the Gospel.

61. The Holy Spirit dwells both in individual believers and in Christ's Church as a whole. On the local level, the Church is expressed in the congregation, those whom the Spirit has called to receive the forgiveness of sins distributed from the pulpit, font, and altar. What tremendous strength and encouragement there is in knowing that, together, as the body of Christ, a local congregation is the Spirit's living temple!

Lesson 6

Paul and Titus

Theme verse: *And besides our own comfort, we rejoiced still more at the joy of Titus, because his spirit has been refreshed by you all.*

2 Corinthians 7:13

Objectives

By the power of the Holy Spirit working through God's Word, we will
- discover the joy Paul receives from the Corinthians;
- learn of Paul's great love for Titus, his brother in Christ;
- see God's Word in action bringing the Corinthians to repentance;
- review the importance of staying obedient to God's Word.

62. As we will see, God graciously provided Paul co-workers, such as Titus, in the Gospel. Joint prayer, fellowship, sufferings, and encouragement all serve to strengthen those who are commissioned to share the Gospel more effectively.

63. Answers will vary. While the Bible is not unfamiliar with itinerant preachers and prophets working alone, the New Testament and Early Church see Gospel work being accomplished with two or more persons. Obvious benefits of "not going it alone" are joint resources and mutual support, among others.

Paul Rejoices over the Corinthians

64. Note Paul's words in 2 Corinthians 7:3, "You are in our hearts, to die together and to live together." These words show the love of Christ for the Corinthians as it is displayed in Paul. The apostle is

willing to die for them. In this way, he reflects the love of Christ (John 15:13; Romans 5:6–8).

65. The Holy Spirit working through the Gospel enabled Paul, even in the midst of his tremendous sufferings, to experience these things. Guide participants to share, on a voluntary basis, how they have experienced or are experiencing the "fruit of the Spirit" (Galatians 5:22–23) even in the midst of their trials and troubles.

Paul and Titus Reunite

66. Titus brings news that the Corinthians long to see Paul again. What a wonderful message this must have been for Paul, who had spent sleepless nights worrying if his Letter and his "painful visit" had upset his relationship with them. Paul credits God for Titus's comforting message (2 Corinthians 7:6).

67. Paul was concerned that his messages had grieved the Corinthians, but now he rejoices that the grieving has brought repentance. Upon receiving Titus's news, Paul's concern turns to great joy. Like Jesus our Lord, Paul—and every believer—experiences the full spectrum of emotion—from grief to joy.

68. Godly grief brings repentance for any wrongdoing. Worldly grief does not bring the same results. This is the same grief Judas felt for betraying Christ. He was sorry for what he had done, but it did not lead to contrition before the Lord. Worldly grief only leads to eternal death, while godly grief, brought about only by repentance and faith, leads to eternal life.

69. Godly sorrow has produced in the Corinthians the desire to come humbly before their God and ask Him to remove their sin. Guide participants in discovering the particular aspects of that desire for reconciliation we see in verse 11.

We see an example of a contrite heart also in Psalm 51. There, David comes before God after being confronted in adultery by the prophet Nathan (see especially Psalm 51:10–12). There is a difference between only being sorrowful for our misdeeds and being truly repentant of them, as we see in David's words and in the lives of the Corinthians.

70. True repentance wrought by the Holy Spirit through the Gospel inspires and enables changes in thoughts and feelings within believers. Among the Corinthians, genuine repentance inspired reverence and an eagerness for justice on the behalf of others. Guide

participants in discussing other ways the Holy Spirit begins to give us new thoughts, words, and deeds through the Gospel.

71. Titus was certainly aware of the turmoil in Corinth—that the congregation was attacking itself from within and that the "super-apostles" were spreading false doctrine. Titus must have been apprehensive as he prepared to travel there at Paul's request, for Paul states that he "boasted about them" to Titus. This was perhaps an attempt to buoy Titus's confidence as he went into an unknown situation. The Corinthian response to Titus encouraged him to trust in God (2 Corinthians 7:13, 15).

72. Perhaps one word, *obedience*, comes to mind (v. 15)—not slavish obedience to a set of rules or laws, but the obedience of faith: Spirit-wrought conversion, repentance, faith in Jesus Christ, and a new attitude on life. The Spirit works powerfully in our lives as well, through the same Gospel proclaimed by Titus and Paul to the Corinthians.

God's Word for Today

73. Answers will vary, but there should be some agreement that the Corinthians were in need of Paul's chastisement and discipline. Some congregational members were tempted to return to lives of sexual misconduct, while others were following the false teachings of the "super-apostles." The Holy Spirit, working through Paul's word of Law and Gospel, brought repentance and forgiveness and the power to live the kind of life that God had already given them in Holy Baptism (Romans 6:1–4).

74. Love gracefully risks rejection for the salvation of others. Paul gladly put his relationship with the Corinthians at risk to tell them of their errors, and God blessed him and them in the process. As Christians, we should also place the truthfulness of God's Word and the Gospel of Christ's love above everything else. Earthly pain lasts only for a little while; the joy of heaven lasts forever.

Lesson 7

Christ's Poverty, Our Wealth

Theme verse: *For you know the grace of our Lord Jesus Christ, that though He was rich, yet for your sake He became poor, so that you by His poverty might become rich.*

2 Corinthians 8:9

Objectives

By the power of the Holy Spirit working through God's Word, we will

- explore the heart of stewardship;
- review Titus's new mission;
- discover the new motivation behind stewardship;
- learn the correct interpretation of Malachi 3:10.

The Grace of Giving

75. Answers will vary. Perhaps giving to the Church is a sensitive subject because money impacts every area of our lives. Or, maybe giving to the Church is a touchy issue because it pertains to the Christian faith. Or even further, maybe some people's strong feelings against even discussing their giving to the Church stem from their own feelings of guilt in this matter. Allow participants to explore different answers.

76. Answers will vary. Perhaps the most obvious reason for misunderstanding Christian stewardship is due to a lack of teaching about what the Bible says on this topic.

Getting to the Heart of Stewardship

77. The church in Thessalonica possessed faith, love, and hope, the three great Christian virtues emphasized in Paul's Letters (Romans 5:2–5; Galatians 5:5–6; Colossians 1:4–5).

78. God's love in Christ powerfully impacted these churches with a deep desire to financially help the poorer Judean congregations even though they themselves were poor (2 Corinthians 8:2). Not only did they give beyond their ability (v. 3), they also pleaded with Paul and his companions to allow them do so (v. 4). Do we likewise possess such an attitude toward Christian giving? If time allows, direct participants to Exodus 36:5–7, wherein we read that God's Old Testament people, in preparing to construct the temple, brought more than enough and even had to be restrained in their giving.

79. God-given faith allowed the Macedonians to offer themselves first to the Lord, trusting that He would provide for their every need, and then to Paul and his companions. Ultimately, God's love in Christ flowed into them and from them to their brothers and sisters in Judea. As 2 Corinthians 8:5 proves, the source of Christian giving is none other than God Himself, freely giving out His grace and mercy through our Lord and Savior, Jesus Christ.

80. Allow participants to discuss the full import of this question. Giving is not so much a matter of writing a check as it is a matter of faith. Faith in Christ clings to God's rich promises to us in Christ. God-given faith desires to be used by God according to His good pleasure and to serve our neighbor in love. When we see that our giving is more a matter of God working through us than us performing a work for God, giving becomes free, spontaneous, and cheerful. Perhaps this is the Gospel-rich element missing in many a Christian's understanding about giving to the Church and to charitable causes.

A New Mission for Titus

81. Titus and his helpers will gather the collection to prevent anyone from saying that Paul is taking money from the Corinthians, in effect using them for his own purpose. This "arms-length" approach would ensure that unfounded rumors were easily refuted.

82. The account in Hebrews asks Christians to find ways to "stir" (inspire) each other. Paul uses the generous gift of the Macedonians to "stir up" the Corinthians. Interestingly, the Macedonians were

originally "stirred up" by the eagerness of the Corinthians to provide aid to Jerusalem Christians. Now, Paul uses the completed Macedonian gift to "stir up" the Corinthians. The excitement and liberality of Gospel-giving is contagious!

The New Motivation behind Stewardship

83. Christian giving is not based on the Law; it is based upon the Gospel and God's grace. We give freely from the bounteous gifts God has provided us. Only this kind of giving can be done "cheerfully," as the previous questions and answers have shown. Ultimately, gifts given to the Church unwillingly, reluctantly, or under compulsion are not even good works in God's sight, because they are motivated by the Law. The various tithes of the Old Testament were commanded by God's Law.

84. In these passages, Paul likens Gospel-giving to sowing seed. The more seed that is sown (liberality), the more harvest that will be gathered (abundance). And as we sow generously, God provides for our ability to do so that results in thanksgiving to Him. The Lord promises to reward Christian giving (Proverbs 19:17; Malachi 3:10; Luke 6:38).

God's Word for Today

85. Although there were several Old Testament tithes (see Numbers 18:21–32; Deuteronomy 14:22–26, 28–29), God's people were also commanded to give a tenth of their income as a tithe to the Lord (Leviticus 27:30). As Christians, we give freely from out of the bounty of God's blessings to us. Jesus did not point to the poor woman's fulfillment of the Old Testament tithe, but to her faith, wherein lies the crux of the matter for Christians. Giving is by God's grace through faith in Christ that results in love, in this case represented by financial giving. The two copper coins the poor woman gave were the equivalent of 1/64 of a denarius, (about a day's wages for a worker). Considering an eight-hour workday, the woman only had about eight minute's pay, or about .64¢ (USA minimum wage, $5.15, 2006). In other words, the woman was extremely poor, but she also had extreme faith that resulted in extreme giving. Oh, that we would have such faith and confidence in our gracious, giving God!

86. Often those who give to so-called "prosperity preachers" expect monetary blessings in return. God makes no such promise. The blessing God promises in Malachi is not specifically revealed to be money. Paul says in 2 Corinthians 9:8–11 that God will enlarge our "harvest of . . . righteousness," that is, strengthen our faith to trust God's promises. God has already richly blessed believers with friends, family, jobs, homes, vehicles, and many other material blessings. Isn't it far more important that God strengthen our trust in Him?

Lesson 8

Obedience to Christ

Theme verse: *We destroy arguments and every lofty opinion raised against the knowledge of God, and take every thought captive to obey Christ.*

2 Corinthians 10:5

Objectives

By the power of the Holy Spirit working through God's Word, we will

- examine how God used Paul's "meekness";
- understand the importance of applying Law and Gospel in winning hearts for Christ;
- compare Paul's ministry to that of the "super-apostles";
- grow in our understanding of obedience to Christ.

More False Accusations

87. Paul was accused of being meek when physically present and bold when he was away. Paul answers that claim by saying that he hopes he doesn't have to show his boldness when he pays the Corinthians a visit. In contrast to his earlier Letter, Paul now "entreats" and "begs" the Corinthians to consider his request. He does so based on the humility—the "meekness and gentleness"—of our Savior, Jesus Christ. He does so in order to spare them from uncharacteristic "boldness" when he arrives later.

88. Perhaps Paul was meek during his first visit with the Corinthians because he was not yet fully aware of their problems. During the second visit (1 Corinthians 2:1–5), Paul was somewhat stern. His second Letter, the one we know today as 1 Corinthians, was

a follow-up to that visit, and it also contains some words of Law. Paul says he wrote it "out of much affliction and anguish" (2 Corinthians 2:4). God provided the power behind the normally meek Paul, who admonished the straying Corinthians in order that they might be brought back to God.

89. The words Paul uses to combat sin are not his own; they are God's Word. Paul is engaged in a spiritual battle for the souls of the Corinthians, and God provides His ammunition in His Law and Gospel. Likewise, our spiritual battles are fought not with fist and gun and sword, but with God's Word, the Sacraments, worship, prayer, and Christian fellowship.

90. Ephesians 6:17 reveals the only offensive spiritual weapon: "the sword of the Spirit, which is the word of God" (see also Hebrews 4:12; Revelation 1:16; 2:12). Many times throughout his missionary career, Paul used God's Word to do battle against Satan. He's about to use it again.

The Power of the Gospel

91. Sinful, that is unregenerate, human reason argues that if salvation is not entirely up to us (through our works or through good works outweighing our bad works) then it is up to us partly. And yet, God's Word says that salvation is entirely by God's grace through faith in Christ. Reason sees Christ as a moral leader or a great man or even someone to be pitied, but God-given faith believes Him to be both God and man, God in human flesh. Reason sees life as all there is and death as the end; the Gospel sees Christ's death as the Christian's forgiveness and Christ's rising to life again as the promise of the Christian's resurrection. Thus, the Gospel, which is received solely by faith, trumps reason's "arguments" and "lofty opinions."

92. In the midst of Paul's weakness was the power of the Gospel: "Jesus Christ and Him crucified" (1 Corinthians 2:2; see also 1:18). Through Paul's preaching, there was a "demonstration of the Spirit and of power, so that [their] faith might not rest in the wisdom of men but in the power of God" (1 Corinthians 2:4–5). Likewise, with Paul "we take captive every thought to make it obedient to Christ," which we do in faith. Our faith rests solely on Him.

93. The first order of business for Paul will be to support and nurture those who have been influenced by the false teachings of the "super-apostles." Paul's second order of business will be to discipline

those who have contradicted his teaching, that is, those who have taught a false gospel and thus a false Christ.

94. Certainly Paul will address the "super-apostles" with the Law. However, he also hopes to address most of the congregation in Corinth with the Gospel. Likewise, pastors, church leaders, and individual Christians should seek to appropriately apply both Law and Gospel. Those who are weak in the faith and repentant need to hear the comforting news that their sins have been paid for by Christ on the cross. All is forgiven. Those who persist in open, unrepentant sin, including unrepentant teaching of false doctrine, need to be told that their sins remain unforgiven, that is, they have lost faith and have driven out the Holy Spirit. The application of Law and Gospel happens generally and publicly on Sunday mornings; it happens privately between two or more Christians or between pastor and penitent.

95. Paul warns his detractors, the "super-apostles," that the very same person who has been bold in his previous Letter to the congregation will be bold with them in person.

Paul's Ministry vs. the "Super-Apostles"

96. Ironically, while the "super-apostles" were bragging about their accomplishments and appealing to the Corinthians through the base wisdom of the world, their vision was cast no further than the city of Corinth. In yet another contrast between God's chosen apostle and those who only claimed to be, Paul's vision was both to minister to the Corinthians and then to expand his Gospel preaching "in lands beyond you" (v. 16). The "super-apostles" were satisfied with gains of position and prominence among the Corinthians; Paul was focused on preaching the message of Christ crucified in Corinth and beyond.

97. All Christians who boast should only boast in the Lord, who has provided all our talents for the furtherance of His kingdom. Success, fame, power, position, numbers, and results are not required of God's servants. However, faithfulness to God's teachings in His Word is (1 Corinthians 4:2).

God's Word for Today

98. Apparently, public speaking was not a natural skill for Paul. But God's grace gave him the knowledge of the mystery of Christ. The Gospel, God's power, energized his feeble words. God's work alone made him an effective minister. Likewise, we can take great comfort in

knowing that God's Word will not return to Him without accomplishing that which He desires (Isaiah 55:11), and that, through the hearing of the Good News of Jesus, God grants faith in His Son (Romans 10:17).

99. Paul refuses to let his intellect run free and become self-serving as has happened to the "super-apostles." Instead, Paul's intellect is "obedient to Christ" or, better still, Christ-serving. This was done through repentance of all human wisdom and opinion and the humble and believing reception of the truth revealed in Jesus Christ through God's Word.

Christianity is not a "mindless" religion; it accepts demonstrable truth from the created order, but rejects claims about that creation that militate against unchanging and errorless divine revelation. We believe in dinosaurs, for example; we have seen their bones. We just don't believe that they evolved; they were created by God. Throughout the past two thousand years, Christians have used their God-given intellect in service to Christ and the Church and in service to the world. Allow participants to discuss how the Gospel can continue to be served through the use of sanctified human reason.

Lesson 9

Different Spirit, Different Gospel

Theme verse: *I betrothed you to one husband, to present you as a pure virgin to Christ.*

2 Corinthians 11:2

Objectives

By the power of the Holy Spirit working through God's Word, we will

- grow in our understanding of Paul's commitment to Christ;
- learn how Paul describes himself in Christ's wedding party and why he wants to protect Christ's bride, the Church;
- recount the sufferings Paul gladly endures;
- discover how faithfully Christ's message of salvation has been handed down to believers today.

Paul: Member of the Wedding Party

100. In John 3:29–30, John the Baptist described himself as a friend of the Bridegroom—perhaps what we might today know as a "best man." In 2 Corinthians 11:1–2, Paul evokes the image of the father of the bride (see 6:13, where he describes the Corinthians as his "children") to help them understand the paternal love and care he is exercising on their behalf.

101. The "super-apostles" are behaving like unwelcome suitors, clamoring after a pure and beautiful woman (the congregation) who is already promised to another man (Christ). Attracting her with pomp and circumstance, flowery words and show, these rogues might

eventually tempt the young lady to let down her guard and be sullied through false teaching. In such a case, having rejected her heavenly Bridegroom, she would not be pure on the day that He came to claim her. Keep in mind that the Bridegroom can come at any time; it is important that the bride always be both pure and prepared to meet her Husband by hearing and believing the pure Gospel. Paul is concerned as the Corinthians' "spiritual father" that his "spiritual daughter," the congregation, be pure and ready to meet the Lord.

Protecting Christ's Bride

102. Satan is the ultimate misogynist; he literally hates women. Satan thought so little of Eve that he robbed her of her trust in God, her Father, and did so while twisting and despising His Word—and this in front of her husband! Satan now abuses the Corinthian congregation as he abused Eve. This time, however, instead of speaking through a serpent, the devil speaks to the congregation through the "super-apostles," who twist God's Word of Gospel, thus attempting to besmirch her in her relationship with her Husband, Christ. And Satan does this in front of her spiritual "father"!

Any gospel that preaches salvation by means apart from the sinless life, sacrificial death, and life-giving resurrection of Jesus Christ is a "different" gospel giving a "different" Jesus and a "different" spirit. In verse 4, Paul ties Jesus, Gospel, and Spirit together. The Holy Spirit works only through the pure Gospel, and only through the pure Gospel do we have the true Jesus. That is why Christian doctrine, Christian teaching, matters. It matters because faith in Jesus Christ is foundational to salvation (John 14:6).

103. Paul is superior in the knowledge of Christ's salvation as revealed by the power of the Holy Spirit. The Corinthians are aware of this as he has demonstrated that God-given knowledge both in preaching and in writing.

104. Actually, Paul was receiving financial support for his Gospel teaching and preaching—just not from the Corinthians! The Macedonians supported him. The charge the "super-apostles" made against him—that he took no money—ultimately was baseless. He had good reason not to take the Corinthians' money, as we will soon see.

105. Paul will continue to refuse financial support from the Corinthians (2 Corinthians 11:12). Why? Because in so doing he will

expose the "false apostles" for what they are: greedy false teachers in league with Satan (vv. 13–15).

106. Ultimately, the "super-apostles" were preaching works-righteousness.

Paul's Apostolic Suffering

107. Paul humbly bears the scars of his faithfulness to Christ. In all probability, before this Letter, Paul has never fully mentioned his sufferings to the Corinthians. He mentions them here only to validate what Christ said would be a mark of his discipleship: suffering (Acts 9:16). Paul has frequently been in prison, been flogged severely, and exposed to death. Five separate times, he has received the traditional Jewish beating of forty lashes minus one. He was stoned, shipwrecked three times, and spent a day in the open sea. He has also been in danger in the countryside, on rivers, on the sea, from bandits, from his fellow Jews, from the Gentiles, and from false brothers. Paul has gone hungry, been cold and naked, and faced daily pressures, all for the sake of the Church. While the "super-apostles" boast about their successes, Paul boasts about his weaknesses (2 Corinthians 11:30).

108. Paul takes no pride in revealing his suffering or his embarrassment. Here he is, an apostle of the Lord Jesus Christ, the very Son of God, and yet he has to escape false arrest like a common criminal (vv. 31–33; Acts 9:23–25)! Indeed, God's power in the Gospel was manifested in Paul's weakness (2 Corinthians 4:7).

God's Word for Today

109. Of course, there are false teachers today, who would lead us away from the true Christ. Paul warns the pastors at Ephesus against the "fierce wolves" that would follow him (see Acts 20:29–31). These same wolves exist today. Satan is defeated, but he still desires to take as many people to hell with him as he can. John exhorts us to "test the spirits" by the Holy Spirit according to the apostolic teaching about Christ, as recorded in Scripture (see 1 John 4:1–6). We know from Jesus that false teachers have the appearance of goodness, but that the fruit they produce is rotten (Matthew 7:15–16). We should be like the Bereans, searching the Scriptures to discern if what we hear from the sanctuary pulpit and classroom lectern are in accordance with the Bible (Acts 17:11). Like the "super-apostles" of Corinth, false teachers of

our day will be marked by greed and heretical doctrines (2 Peter 2:1–3).

110. Paul claims in 1 Corinthians that the message he received, he has passed on to the Corinthians. That message includes that "*Christ died for our sins . . .* , that He was *buried,* [and] that He was *raised on the third day,*" all according to Holy Scripture (1 Corinthians 15:3–4, emphasis added). Paul also claims that if we do not believe that Christ was *raised from the dead,* then we remain in our sin.

In the Apostles' Creed, we read: "*[I believe] in Jesus Christ,* His only Son, our Lord, who was conceived by the Holy Spirit, born of the virgin Mary, . . . was *crucified, died* and was *buried.* He descended into hell. The third day *He rose again from the dead.* He ascended into heaven and sits at the right hand of God the Father Almighty. From thence He will come to judge the living and the dead" (italics added).

Notice how the italicized words in Paul's text match those in the Apostles' Creed. This is the same message of salvation. Allow participants to discuss how this Creed might be useful when we share our Christian faith with someone who does not yet know the Lord.

Lesson 10

Sufficient Grace

Theme verse: *But He said to me, "My grace is sufficient for you, for My power is made perfect in weakness."*

2 Corinthians 12:9

Objectives

By the power of the Holy Spirit working through God's Word, we will
- discover the vision of heaven God gave Paul;
- discuss Paul's "thorn in the flesh" and God's sufficient grace;
- explore the three marks of a true apostle;
- grow in appreciation of how God's grace is sufficient for our lives.

Caught Up into Heaven

111. Paul's experience was unusual, singular, and real. In describing being bodily "caught up" (2 Corinthians 12:2), Paul uses the same word as he does in 1 Thessalonians 4:17, which speaks of believers being bodily "caught up" with Jesus when He returns on the Last Day. Having seen this heavenly vision, Paul was strengthened for service. Through faith and by God's Word, we know what lies in store for us as believers. In the words of the Nicene Creed, we "look for the resurrection of the dead and the life of the world to come."

112. Although God gave Paul a wondrous revelation of heaven, he chose not to speak about it so that he would not appear to be boasting (2 Corinthians 12:6). Paul did not want the Corinthians to regard him as anything more than a humble servant of God's Word. Unlike the "super-apostles," Paul's ministry pointed to Christ; the ministry of the "super-apostles" pointed only to themselves. Part of

what Paul heard in heaven was so exalted that he was not permitted by God to disclose it (v. 4).

113. Acts 16:9–10 describes Paul's vision while in Troas, in which he saw a man from Macedonia begging him to come to Macedonia and "help them." This was God's message to Paul calling him to take God's ministry of reconciliation to Macedonia. Following that vision, Paul established congregations in Thessalonica, Berea, and Philippi. Acts 18:9–11 mentions a vision Paul had while staying in Corinth. In that vision, God told Paul that He would protect him from attack and harm while he established a congregation there. In response, Paul remained in Corinth for eighteen months.

114. By now it should be clear that Paul wanted the Corinthians to rely fully and solely on God's grace through Christ—to rely fully on the Gospel for which he suffered so much on their behalf.

God's Grace Is Sufficient

115. God gave Paul this ailment or condition in order to keep him from becoming conceited—so great and marvelous was his experience. God allowed Satan to play a role in delivering this suffering to Paul (see Job 2:6–7, where the Lord allows Satan, within God's clear boundaries, to afflict Job).

116. Although Paul asked God to remove the thorn three times, each time God's response was no. God's grace was sufficient. God was accomplishing great things through Paul's weaknesses. Whatever this thorn was, it kept Paul on his knees seeking God's strength to endure another hour, another day. Through Paul's many weaknesses, God brought many people to faith. Would that we would have the same attitude—to choose obedient suffering rather than disobedient pleasure.

117. Jesus calls His followers blessed when they are poor, mournful, and meek (Matthew 5:1–12). Like Paul, He Himself prayed for His suffering to be taken away three times (26:36–46). Yet, He also prayed, "Your will be done" (v. 42). This is our prayer too, as His disciples (Matthew 6:10). No servant is greater than his master (John 13:16; 15:20). If Jesus suffered in His earthly life, then we can expect suffering as well. This biblical teaching stands in sharp contrast to contemporary "health and wealth" preachers and teachers, who, like the "super-apostles," deliver a false gospel and a false Christ.

118. God's grace gave him the strength to endure the thorn that God had given him (2 Corinthians 12:9). Paul willingly endured

hardships because of the hope of eternal life offered through Jesus Christ's death and resurrection (2 Timothy 1:8–12). We do likewise.

119. Answers will vary. If time permits, allow participants to break off into groups of two or three for this personal time of sharing. Personal experiences could then be shared with the larger group on a voluntary basis.

Paul Anticipates His Return to Corinth

120. Jesus describes a variety of gifts given to the apostles in order to support their ministries (Mark 16:14–20; Luke 9:1–2). Paul describes the three marks of a true apostle as "signs and wonders and mighty works," or miracles (2 Corinthians 12:12; see also Romans 15:18–19). Additionally, Paul taught that another mark of an apostle is the fruit of his ministry (that is, faith in Jesus Christ that comes into the lives of unbelievers). True apostles like Paul commended themselves through their endurance; true apostles were servants, not show-offs; and true apostles suffered much to carry their message of salvation to others. In essence, Jesus' true apostles were everything the "super-apostles" weren't.

121. Certainly any pastor today is humbled by impenitence in his flock, just as Paul was likewise burdened by the impenitence of the Corinthians. The burdens of the pastoral ministry, and Church ministry in general, are tremendous. However, God uses these burdens to keep His ministers looking to Him for help and guidance.

God's Word for Today

122. Answers will vary. Paul's primary message in this Letter to the Corinthians was a message of comfort (2 Corinthians 1:3–6). God invites us to call upon Him in our times of trouble and trust Him to deliver us (Psalm 50:15). That is a solemn promise from the God who loved us so much that He sent His Son to pay the penalty our sins deserved. Guide participants in discussing practical ways they have or they could provide assistance to congregational members or others that are suffering hardships.

Lesson 11

The God of Love and Peace

Theme verse: *For He [Christ] was crucified in weakness, but lives by the power of God.*

2 Corinthians 13:4

Objectives

By the power of the Holy Spirit working through God's Word, we will

- compare Corinth and our society today;
- review Paul's renewed call to repentance;
- acquaint ourselves with the meaning of Paul's trinitarian benediction;
- discover ways to apply this lesson to the society in which we live.

A New Call to Repentance

123. Old Testament Law required the testimony of two or three witnesses in a legal or criminal matter. Under the Holy Spirit's guidance, Paul reiterates that requirement here. Having multiple, preferably disinterested (witnesses without a cause in the dispute) ensures that matters can be handled more fairly. Especially in the Church, when not only temporal but also eternal lives are at stake, every effort must be made to restore sinners patiently and fairly. Exercising Christian love, without compromising God's truth recorded in the Bible, is a difficult matter. However, for the sake of the faith of those inside the Church, and as a witness to those outside the Church, such patience and fairness need to be exercised.

124. Answers will vary. Obviously, a second or third witness provides a greater likelihood that evidence can be corroborated should

110

something happen to one of the witnesses. Also, by requiring two or three witnesses to substantiate a claim, the likelihood of a false accusation being made is greatly lessened. Marriage licenses require multiple witnesses, as do many other legal documents.

125. The two groups Paul wants addressed are: (a) those who continue in their past sins, and (b) all others who willfully fall into new sins. Paul is clearly warning both groups that they must repent before he arrives in Corinth. If they do not, Paul will administer God's justice. Paul's example is an excellent model for congregations to follow.

126. Christ became weak (submitted to His own humiliation) when, as God, He could have removed Himself from the cross. However, through His weakness, Christ earned our salvation (see Isaiah 53:2–3; Philippians 2:8). Paul is likewise weak; he even boasts in his weaknesses. Nevertheless, Christ powerfully defeated death, hell, and the devil on the cross—His point of weakness. And through the Gospel—that is, the proclamation of Christ's life, death, and resurrection in Paul's weak words—the Gospel was powerfully demonstrated. Thus, for both Christ and Paul, God's power was made perfect in human weakness (see 2 Corinthians 12:9).

127. The Corinthians will find all the evidence they need to prove that Jesus Christ is in them: they trust in Him as their Savior and Lord. In addition, their deeds confirm the power of God's work through Paul's Gospel proclamation, for the Corinthians are Paul's "letter . . . known and read by all" (2 Corinthians 3:2). The Corinthians know that the Holy Spirit is at work in them if the words "Jesus is Lord" are believed in their hearts and flow from their lips (Romans 10:9; 1 Corinthians 12:3). Such a confession is only possible by the power of the Holy Spirit.

128. Paul tells the Corinthians that he is praying for their "restoration" with God, that is, their being made whole and useful again for His purposes.

129. Though the preaching of Law is necessitated by sin, it is the Gospel that Paul desires to minister. This is his goal for his forthcoming visit: to proclaim to them God's Yes! in Jesus Christ (1:18–20), which is his God-given duty (2:17); to minister to them the new covenant of the Gospel of Christ's blood (3:6–11), which is the ministry of reconciliation; and to preach to them that God has reconciled them to Himself through Christ (5:18–20), which is their very salvation (6:1–2).

Paul's Closing and Trinitarian Benediction

130. Here we see Paul's love for the Corinthians. Having earlier considered them his spiritual daughter, he now looks upon them as though he was their brother.

131. Repentance and restoration to God through the true Gospel of Christ have been Paul's pressing concerns throughout this Letter. As he is Christ's chosen and sent apostle, it is important that they hear, understand, and obey his teachings. Because their society and, in turn, their congregation fell prey so easily to smooth and divisive teachers, they would by God's grace have to focus on maintaining unity in the true teaching of the Gospel. Paul assures them that the "God of love and peace" will be with them in that task.

132. As they greeted each other with a "holy kiss," perhaps a reference to the custom maintained within the liturgy of the Lord's Supper, they would recognize that they were not alone—they had each other. Likewise, Paul reminds them that there are other saints—those in Macedonia and those in Judea, for example—who also greet them. The Corinthian congregation was not alone in its faith.

133. With this benediction, Paul invokes the name of the triune God: God's grace through Jesus Christ, God's (the Father's) love, and the Holy Spirit's fellowship. God's grace, love, and fellowship are exactly what the congregation needed, and through this benediction, which is still heard in Christian churches today, God gives it.

134. Answers will vary. Guide participants in a discussion of how they have witnessed each of these gifts in their congregation, and how they might be shared in their community.